# ☆ TRAINING
# ☆ THE SMALL
# ☆ DEPARTMENT

*By*

## JAMES H. AUTEN B.S., M.Ed.

*University of Illinois*
*Police Training Institute*
*Champaign, Illinois*

CHARLES C THOMAS • PUBLISHER
*Springfield • Illinois • U.S.A.*

*Published and Distributed Throughout the World by*

CHARLES C THOMAS • PUBLISHER

Bannerstone House

301-327 East Lawrence Avenue, Springfield, Illinois, U.S.A.

©*1973, by* CHARLES C THOMAS • PUBLISHER

ISBN 0-398-02719-6

Library of Congress Catalog Card Number: 72-92160

*Printed in the United States of America*

*R-1*

Dedicated to my parents
who made this possible.

# INTRODUCTION

As the development of law enforcement in the United States progresses from its early forms toward the self-professed goal of professionalization, more and more emphasis is being placed on education and training for the modern law enforcement officer. Within the last ten years our society has been subject to significant changes the effect of which have been felt by law enforcement. Law enforcement, along with many other social institutions, reflects this changing society in its method of operation. This method of operation should additionally reflect the aims and concerns of the society being served by law enforcement. Unfortunately, in many instances the aims and concerns of society are unclear. As a result, the function of law enforcement in today's society is unclear, and law enforcement administrators are in a quandry as to what the public really wants in terms of law enforcement.

In one respect law enforcement's answer to this dilemma has been an increased emphasis on law enforcement education and training. The last ten years have literally been the scene of an *explosion* in the fields of law enforcement training and education. The federal government, state governments, and the larger metropolitan areas, along with educational institutions, have entered into the areas of education and training with an increasing vigor.

Unfortunately, in many instances this involvement has created a vacuum around the smaller law enforcement agencies in the United States. Smaller law enforcement agencies simply do not, in many instances, possess the personnel or technological expertise to become actively involved in training. They lack qualified personnel to act as instructors, to prepare grant requests or to properly develop and administer meaningful training programs. Many police administrators of smaller law enforcement agencies use this deficiency as an excuse for their lack of trained personnel.

While this view is commonly expressed, it has no real basis in fact. Few people, based upon native ability alone, are qualified to perform in the varied roles required of those involved in police training. The fact is that the required skills and knowledge can be learned by the individual. Personnel can learn to instruct, prepare grant requests and perform the administrative tasks related to training. Many administrators are actively interested in training but feel that it is beyond their existing resources.

The purpose of this text is to provide guidelines for the administrator of the smaller police department to follow when developing the training function of his department. Any police department, regardless of its resources, can become involved in training in a successful manner if certain basic principles are followed. If the advancement of law enforcement toward the elusive goal of professionalization is to continue, then all law enforcement organizations must be improved. To neglect the smaller law enforcement agency is to care for the exposed portion of a plant while neglecting the roots. These smaller law enforcement organizations form the *backbone* of law enforcement in this country and in the end will be the yardstick against which our efforts toward professionalization will be measured.

# CONTENTS

# TRAINING IN
# THE SMALL
# DEPARTMENT

*Chapter I*

# CURRENT TRENDS IN LAW ENFORCEMENT TRAINING AND EDUCATION

*No person, regardless of his individual qualifications, is prepared to perform police work on native ability alone. Aside from the individual intelligence, prior education, judgement and emotional fitness, an officer must receive extensive vocational training before he can understand the police task and learn how to fulfill it.\**

THIS quote represents a fact of life which an increasing number of law enforcement personnel are becoming aware of daily. Not only are administrators becoming aware of this situation, but so are other law enforcement personnel right down to the man on the beat. The operational level officer is beginning to expect training and resents it when he is not afforded the opportunity to develop to his full potential. Today's recruit police officer is more intelligent, better educated, and more aware of his environment than was the recruit officer five years ago.

If law enforcement is to attract the most qualified personnel into its ranks, then it must offer the individual an opportunity to develop his latent abilities to the fullest. Too many qualified personnel leave law enforcement because they feel their personal development has been restricted. It seems that every time a police department loses a good officer the consensus is that he left for a better paying job. While financial rewards certainly influence a persons choice of employment, other factors are involved. The vast majority of those entering law enforcement are well aware of

---

*\*Task Force Report: The Police.* The President's Commission on Law Enforcement and Administration of Justice, U.S. Government Printing Office, Washington D.C., 1967, p. 137.

the compensation involved. They are nontheless willing to accept this frequently low level of compensation in view of other rewards such as job satisfaction, promotional opportunities and opportunities for training and education. No longer can law enforcement expect to hire qualified personnel who will be satisfied to patrol a beat for twenty years and then retire at the rank of patrolman.

In terms of the priorities facing law enforcement, the need for well-trained law enforcement officers has grown rapidly within the past ten years. To meet this ever-increasing need many states have acted by legislating requirements concerning police training. According to a survey conducted by the International Association of Chiefs of Police, seventeen states have mandatory training for recruit or entry-level police officers and fourteen states have voluntary entry-level training. In addition, three states have mandated supervisory-management level training and three states have made in-service training mandatory.*

This expansion involving the training of law enforcement officers has been complemented by an increasing number of educational programs at the college and university level. Evidence of this expansion has been most evident at the junior college level. Between 1961 and 1968, junior colleges increased their programs in general 40.1 per cent, while junior college law enforcement programs increased 306.1 per cent during the same period. In addition, while enrollment in junior colleges in general increased 60.1 per cent between 1964 and 1967, the enrollment in junior college law enforcement programs increased 147.2 per cent during the same period. Junior college involvement in the field of law enforcement education has reached the point that in 1968 there were 199 institutions in the United States offering Associate of Arts degrees relating to law enforcement.† This increased involvement of the junior colleges in law enforcement education is further reflected by the increasing number of police officers to be found in the classroom during off-duty time.

This growth of junior college programs relating to law

---

*The Police Chief. International Association of Chiefs of Police, Washington D.C., August 1968, pp. 76-77.
†Crockett, Thompson S.: *Law Enforcement Education*. International Association of Chiefs of Police, Washington D.C., 1968, p. 1.6.

enforcement has been accompanied by an increase in baccalaureate and graduate degree programs relating to law enforcement. In some instances existing programs have been expanded, and in others disciplines such as sociology and psychology have been modified to better meet the needs of those interested in law enforcement.

During the period between 1958 and 1968, law enforcement programs at the baccalaureate and graduate levels grew 207.7 per cent. In conjunction with this expansion at least forty-eight colleges and universities offered a total of sixty-two programs leading to the award of bachelors, masters, and doctors degrees in the law enforcement field.* These expanding facilities offer today's law enforcement officer opportunities for training and education that did not exist ten years ago.

In spite of this increased awareness of the roles that training and education play in the development of today's law enforcement officers, the administrators of many smaller police organizations are still faced with the same problems that confronted them ten years ago. If anything, this increased awareness has only served to amplify these existing problems and to create a situation demanding their solution. While training and education cannot be looked upon as an absolute panacea for the problems facing law enforcement, they are an all-important first step.

Within smaller police organizations one of the initial problems facing the administrator concerning the improvement of the organization through training rests with the number of personnel within the organization. For example: If the entire organization only consists of ten members, then to send three of them away to receive training will most certainly create hardships for the remainder of the organization. Two obvious solutions come to mind: either send only one officer at a time away to school, or conduct the needed training within the organization itself. In this regard the administrator should recognize departmental in-service training will have to be conducted as an adjunct to any academy training.

Another area of immediate concern to the administrator relates

----

*Ibid.*, p. 1.9.

to the funds available for the training of personnel. According to a survey conducted by the International Association of Chiefs of Police, nine states make some form of financial reimbursement to law enforcement agencies relating to training received. In the majority of these instances the police organization or political subdivision is reimbursed up to 50 per cent of the involved officers salary along with 50 per cent of his living and travel expenses.*

In spite of these measures, financing training continues to be a problem for police administrators. This is because many of the organizations in the past have had neither the interest nor involvement in the training of departmental personnel. In the past communities served by these organizations were apparently satisfied with the level of police service they received. Such may no longer be the case. The roles of education and training are not only becoming readily apparent to law enforcement personnel, but also the awareness of the general public is increasing. Administrators of law enforcement organizations who previously have not been involved in training must be prepared to request budget allocations and begin planning at the lowest levels.

With the ever-increasing complexity of our society and the resultant increasing demands being placed upon law enforcement, the modern law enforcement officer must be trained, if only at the minimum level, just to meet the public's expectations. These demands being placed upon law enforcement almost certainly will not decrease in the years to come, and law enforcement cannot afford to mark time anymore. Responsive and responsible law enforcement administrators will recognize that this is the trend in law enforcement training and education and will respond accordingly.

Even though the administrator of the smaller police organization feels either sending away of personnel to receive additional training or limited funding severely limits his ability to provide his personnel with needed training, the principles set forth in this text may be implemented at a moderate cost. The following quote best summarizes the overall responsibility facing the law enforcement administrator:

*The Police Chief.* International Association of Chiefs of Police, Washington D.C., August 1968, p. 78.

For there to be basic improvement, it is essential that the legitimacy of the training needs be recognized. There ought not to be any hesitation or reluctance on the part of police administrators or the public to support police training. It should be viewed as a vital and indispensible process in equipping a police officer to perform highly sensitive and complex functions. It ought also to be recognized as a continuing need. Training cannot be accomplished by occasional programs and improvised programs. Rather there is need for established programs, qualified staffs, and adequate physical facilities.*

In response to society's demands and the need for the acceptance of the previously cited responsibilities, the trend in law enforcement training is toward a minimum standard of training. In addition, there is an increasing emphasis on the need to ensure that every police officer receives the specialized training that is essential to the successful performance of his duties.

There are continuing indications that the role of education in upgrading law enforcement is becoming increasingly recognized. Many law enforcement agencies have raised their entrance requirements to include some college education or a bachelors degree. Other agencies have followed the example set by business organizations and gone to the college or university campus to recruit qualified applicants. Still other agencies have reached the stage where some degree of advanced education is required to hold supervisory and management positions. Finally, some agencies have arranged to partially defray the educational expenses of personnel or to provide a pay differential for advanced education.

These types of activities have resulted in the entrance into law enforcement of a *new breed* of young police officers. This influx of intelligent, inquisitive and social-conscious young officers has further served to emphasize the need for education and training. In many instances these officers who have been exposed to the college environment desire to continue their education after entering law enforcement. Additionally, their desire to continue their advanced studies is contagious to other members of the organization in that they become aware of the significance of a college education in law enforcement and may desire to begin

*Task Force Report: The Police. The President's Commission on Law Enforcement and Administration of Justice, U.S. Government Printing Office, Washington D.C., 1967, p. 37.

their college careers.

The advent of college-trained officers has served to emphasize the need for training. Even though the college-trained police officer may be academically qualified to assume the law enforcement role, he is usually lacking in those practical skills and specific knowledge so essential to a successful law enforcement effort. To neglect to provide this essential training to these young men will only create disappointment and frustration within them. It is this disappointment and frustration that causes otherwise well-qualified personnel to leave law enforcement, not low pay as is so often voiced.

Law enforcement agencies have only recently begun to use some of the available educational and training hardware. The use of videotape equipment in providing the vehicle for in-service training is growing rapidly and new applications to law enforcement are being revealed almost daily. In addition, other forms of educational technology such as teaching machines, programmed instruction, various teaching methods, and audiovisual equipment are being adopted for use in law enforcement training.

Not only have law enforcement agencies become more actively involved in training, but also law enforcement support organizations, such as the International Association of Chiefs of Police, have become actively involved in developing and providing the support materials for training programs. In addition to providing these support materials, many organizations of this type offer to travel to the concerned law enforcement organization to provide the specialized in-service training. The growth of education and training as related to law enforcement is just beginning and the years to come can only provide more advancements to assist in the meaningful growth of law enforcement.

# Chapter II

# MANAGEMENT RESPONSIBILITIES
# TO THE TRAINING FUNCTION

W HEN discussing the management responsibilities of a police organization to the training function it is essential to understand this responsibility originates at the highest administrative level and continues down to the supervisory level. Naturally, those responsibilities at the highest administrative level are more complex and far-reaching than those at the supervisory level; however, if the training function within the organization is to be successful the importance of each level, administrative, command and supervisory, cannot be over-emphasized. If there is a failure to accept or discharge the appropriate responsibilities at any of these levels, the entire training function will suffer.

The responsibilities of those at the administrative level within the police organization fall into two general areas: the responsibilities to the general public and the responsibilities to the police organization itself. Of these two, those responsibilities to the general public are probably the most strongly felt by those at the administrative level. After all, in the final analysis, the chief administrator must answer to the public for the activities of his subordinates.

The administrator's responsibilities to the general public are to a large extent predicated upon the public's expectations concerning the organization. An additional source of responsibility to the general public arises from the administrator's own feelings as to what level of performance he can, in good conscience, afford to provide the public. In many cases, it may well be that the chief administrator's concept of an acceptable performance level will exceed the expectations of the general public. In cases of this type he has the problem of convincing the public and the administration of local government that his level of performance desired is one that should be shared by all within the community. It is most likely that a conflict of this nature will arise when the chief requests additional funding to establish and support the training necessary to bring the performance level up to this desired standard.

In this period of social unrest and change one of the most complex problems facing the chief administrator is to determine, as precisely as is possible, what the expectations of the general public are concerning the police operation. One of the frequent criticisms of pressure groups within our society is related to the demand for change. Unfortunately, in many instances they fail to delineate just how this desired change is to be accomplished. Concerning the police operation, what may well be an acceptable performance level to one segment of the society may be totally unacceptable to another segment. Realistically speaking, about the most the police administrator can hope to accomplish is to satisfy most of the people most of the time.

The process of actually determining the public's expectations can be approached in several ways. The first of these is for representatives of the police organization to meet and discuss with groups of citizens the role of the police organization within the community. The citizens should be directly solicited for their opinions concerning the current police operation within the community and how they feel that it may be improved. In an operation of this type it becomes essential that all levels of the community be contacted and their opinions sought. In the event that recommendations of citizens are implemented, the public should be advised of the implementation and how it is going to improve the police operation. Whenever recommendations from the general public are sought and received, they should be acknowledged. If a recommendation should be deemed unacceptable, then the reasons for its being so should be fully explained.

A second method of operation in this area of concern is to review the number and nature of complaints made by citizens against members of the organization. A constant or ever-increasing flow of complaints from the public concerning the manner in which members of the organization conduct traffic stops would serve to indicate that the organization is not meeting the public's expectations in this area. Frequently reoccurring complaints of discrimination by responsible members of the public against members of the organization would further serve to indicate again that the expectations of the public are not being met. While in some instances citizen's complaints may originate with *cranks* or those who seem to constantly criticize the police operation, many complaints will originate from those who are sincere in their criticism of the police operation. In some cases the degree of provocation required to cause a citizen to make a formal criticism of the police operation will have to be quite extreme. Complaints of this nature should be carefully investigated since they most likely have some basis in fact.

Another area in which the chief administrator can engender feed-back concerning the public's expectations regarding the police operation is in his relationships with the administration of local government. Hopefully, the responsible public official will be reflecting the public's expectations in the manner in which he administers his office. Public officials may receive comments concerning the police operation from their constituents, and these should be of interest to the chief administrator of the police organization.

The responsibilities of the chief administrator to the members of his organization are closely linked to the expectations of the general public. If the general public expects a certain level of performance, then the chief administrator must equip his subordinates to fulfil this expectation. The day when a man could be given a badge and gun and be expected to function satisfactorily as a police officer has long since passed from view. The demands placed upon today's law enforcement officers are continually increasing in complexity and variety. One can only speculate as to the nature of the demands that will be placed upon law enforcement officers in the future, but almost certainly they will not diminish. The responsible police administrator should be aware of these trends and must take the appropriate steps to ensure that his personnel will be equipped to meet this challenge.

When viewing his responsibilities to the training function the chief administrator should have certain objectives in mind. He should view the training function as a process whereby the organization can aid its members in becoming more effective in their present or future positions. To increase a man's effectiveness in the performance of his job not only increases the overall efficiency of the organization, but it also frees the individual to devote attention to other tasks. Naturally, if the training function is to also serve in preparing members of the organization for future tasks, the chief administrator must have some concept of the future needs of the organization.

A second objective for the administrator to consider concerning the training function is that through training he can improve and increase the skills and knowledge of the organizational members. Through this improvement of skills and knowledge, he can help to provide his subordinates with the necessary tools to meet the challenges and demands of modern law enforcement. Once again the administrator's responsibility to properly prepare his subordinates to discharge their duties and responsibilities comes to the fore. The administrator cannot expect his subordinates to properly function unless their skills and knowledge have been developed to a satisfactory level.

Another objective relating to the chief administrator's responsibility to the organization concerns itself with improving the habits of thought and action of his subordinates. Police officers, like everyone else, form patterns of conduct and thinking, whether good or bad, that can stifle self-improvement. As rapidly as the police operation is changing, the responsible administrator cannot afford to let his subordinates stagnate in outdated habits and thoughts.

Directly or indirectly, the administrator, as a result of his organization's training programs, can mold or influence the attitudes of his subordinates. He has the responsibility, through the training function, of ensuring that his subordinates are properly oriented toward law enforcement in general, and in particular, toward the role of his law enforcement organization within the community. In conjunction with this general attitude development, he must develop a favorable attitude toward the training function among the members of his organization as well as the administrators of local government. If the administrator can develop a favorable attitude toward the training function within members of the organization, half the battle of making training a successful and meaningful operation will be won.

Another objective the administrator should have in mind when viewing his responsibilities to the training function is to increase the overall efficiency and proficiency of the organization and its members. Hopefully, as the proficiency of the individuals within the organization increases in the performance of their jobs, so will the overall efficiency of the organization. As these two factors increase, the organization should be able to more fully satisfy the demands placed upon it by society. In addition, it is an advantage for the administrator to be able to tell the public they are getting their money's worth so far as the operation of the police department is concerned.

Perhaps the most important responsibility facing those at the administrative level is to recognize the legitimacy of the training function within the police organization and to support the training programs of the organization. Without this support and recognition of the training function and its attendant programs, the training within the organization will fade into nothingness. As a side effect of this recognition and support at the administrative level, those at the command and supervisory levels will be encouraged to lend their support and recognition to the training function. This support and recognition at all management levels is a necessary ingredient to the success of the training process.

This support and recognition can be manifested in several ways. The first of these is for the administrator to encourage individual and/or group involvement. For example: group involvement could include the formulation of a study group to become involved in the need determination process, and individual involvement as instructors for specific units of instruction. This involvement would include departmental personnel not only taking part in the various training programs as students, but also becoming involved in the entire training process. There is a need for organizational personnel to become involved in the need-determination process, the planning of the training programs to meet these needs, the actual presentation of the training programs and the evaluation process. The larger the number of departmental personnel involved in the training function, and here I am referring to meaningful involvement, the better the understanding of it. Meaningful involvement means the actual, productive involvement in the training process rather than peripheral involvement. Once an individual has contributed to a process he has a vested interest in the successful application of his contributions. In addition, it is difficult to criticize or fail to support a process when we have contributed to that process. Meaningful involvement means when we solicit an individual's contributions to a process, we must in turn consider them carefully and make use of them whenever possible.

Also, when speaking of encouraging individual and/or group involvement it is wise to consider the development of a desire for individual self-improvement. If an individual or individuals have expressed a desire to improve themselves through attendance at a specialized outside training facility, their involvement should be encouraged if at all possible. The frequent refusal of requests of this nature only serves to influence the entire department's training programs in a negative manner. Likewise, if a member of the organization has the desire to instruct in a particular subject area then he should be encouraged to do so.

Another way in which an administrator can display recognition and support for the training function is by utilizing the skills and/or knowledge gained as a result of training. All to frequently an officer receives specialized training and then is not afforded an opportunity to put into practice what he has learned. Once a man has developed proficiency in a particular area, such as firearms, first-aid, traffic crash investigation, or principles of management, let him display this proficiency. As an administrator you can do yourself or your organization no greater disservice than to spend time and money training personnel and then not to reap the benefits of that training.

Finally, the administrator can display support and recognition for the training function by providing the means whereby the training can be accomplished. The means necessary to support the training function fall into three general areas: (a) budget, (b) staff and (c) physical. With regard to budgeting funds for the support of the training function, funds should be made available to finance not only intradepartmental training programs, but also training at specialized outside training facilities. The possibility that you will not be able to meet all the training needs of the organization internally must be taken into account when allocating funds. Naturally, if the training efforts of the organization have been marginal in the past then the administrator must be prepared to document or *sell* the need for additional funding. One obvious way to obtain the necessary documentation is to have a professional organization survey the needs of the organization. Even though the organization may have been actively involved in training, the administrator would be well advised to remember the *battle of the budget* is an annual struggle and documentation for all requested funding will normally be required.

With regard to staffing the training section of the organization, the initial step is to select someone from within the organization to assume the responsibility for training, i.e. a departmental training officer. In addition to the selection of an individual to serve as the departmental training officer, individuals should be assigned to assist him as the need arises. The selection of the training officer should be the end result of the careful considera- tion of potentially qualified personnel. If the responsibility for training is to be vested in one person then it should be realized that this one individual can make or break training within the organization. Suffice it to say, the individual who assumes the responsibility for departmental training must be a person in whom the chief administrator has the utmost confidence.

If the organization anticipates that it is going to conduct courses of instruction on a regular basis, such as training at the recruit or basic level, then it may be advantageous to select a core group of instructors. This group would be assigned to the instruction role in addition to their regularly assigned duties and responsibilities. If the organization is to undertake the basic or recruit-level training of its own personnel, then qualified instruc- tors from within the organization can enhance the learning process since they can relate the training being received specifically to the parent organization. Naturally, an endeavor of this type is predicated upon the assumption that somewhere along the line the instructors have experienced the instructional role or have been trained in its complexities.

In connection with the staffing responsibility the chief administrator needs to ensure that adequate time is allotted to the training
function. Time must not only be allotted in which to actually
conduct the training programs, but it also must be allocated for
the preparation phases that preceed any successful training effort.
The training needs of the organization must be determined, a
priority established among the needs, curriculums must be devised
and agreed upon, the instructional staff selected, and evaluation
techniques devised before the actual training program is presented.
Once the training program has been completed, time must be
allotted in which to evaluate and refine the training program. The
administrative head should realize that much more time is required
to get a meaningful training program off the ground than is
actually spent in presenting the program.

Finally, there is the need to provide adequate physical facilities
in which the training can take place. Under ideal conditions there
should be no need to seek outside facilities in which to conduct
training programs. At a very minimum the organization should
provide a classroom in which the instruction can take place. If the
organization cannot provide the physical space in which to
conduct training programs, then efforts should be made to locate
space elsewhere within the community. A mere lack of space
within the department should never prevent the presentation of
the needed training. In addition, the necessary equipment, such as
visual aids, projectors and chalkboards, which are indigenous to an
educational operation, should be provided by the organization.
Once again, should the organization be unable to provide the
necessary support materials, then the resources of the local
community should be utilized.

As previously mentioned, the responsibilities of those at the
management level do not cease to exist with the administrative
head of the organization. The management responsibility to the
training function continues down through the command and
supervisory levels. At these two levels there also exists, as at the
administrative level, two general areas of responsibility. Those at
the command and supervisory levels still have a responsibility to
the general public; however, it is an indirect responsibility. While
the administrative head is directly responsible to the public for the

actions of his subordinates, those at the command and supervisory levels are directly responsible to the next higher individual in the departmental chain of command rather than the public directly. This is not to say that a responsibility to the public does not exist at these levels because it certainly does. It is the same basic responsibility that all public employees have to their employer, the public in general.

Perhaps the most important or most direct responsibility facing those at the command and supervisory levels concerning the training function is the responsibility to the organization itself. This responsibility takes two forms, involvement and support. Personnel at the command and supervisory levels need to become as directly involved in the training process as is possible. Through this involvement in the various facets of the training function, they will be better able to lend overall support not only to the training function in general, but also to the individual training programs in particular. Unless those at the command and supervisory levels are in some manner directly involved in the training process, it will be most difficult for them to explain the training function to their subordinates.

This involvement on the part of command and supervisory personnel can take several forms, some of which will require the necessary direct involvement. One of the initial steps concerning the training function is the selection of an individual to serve as the departmental training officer. Since it is quite likely personnel from both levels will be candidates for the position and the opinions of members of both levels, particularly at the command level, will be sought before the final selection is made, they are directly involved in that phase of the operation. Their involvement in this initial phase is essential since it affords the administrator an opportunity to demonstrate his intention to involve all departmental personnel in the training function. In essence the chief administrator is making a commitment to total departmental involvement in the training function. As before, it is extremely important that the chief administrator give the appropriate consideration and action to those opinions received.

The next phase in the training program development is the need-determination process. Once again both the command and supervisory level personnel should be directly involved. Those at the supervisory level should be the most qualified to assist in the identification of the training needs at the operational level. This is true of course because supervisory level personnel are in daily contact with operational level employees and are directly responsible for the manner in which they perform their duties. Their daily inspections and evaluations of their subordinates' performance places them in an ideal position to determine operational level training needs. Those at the supervisory level should also be of assistance in identifying some of the training needs at the higher management levels. Since they are charged with the implementation and explanation of decisions reached at higher management levels, they should soon become cognizant of some of the deficiencies at the higher management levels.

While those at the command level may be of assistance in identifying training needs at the operational level, their assistance in singling out training needs at the supervisory level should be most significant. Since they are in almost daily contact with supervisory level personnel and are directly responsible for their level of performance, they should be aware of the supervisory level training needs. As with supervisory level personnel, the relationship of command personnel within the chain of command places them in an ideal position to identify supervisory level training needs. In addition, command personnel can be of assistance in identifying needs at the command and administrative levels to some degree: however, introspection of one's own deficiencies is no more a trait in police personnel than it is in other occupations.

Finally, concerning the need-determination process, the chief administrator must realize he is going to be primarily responsible for determining the training needs of command level personnel. Realizing the deficiencies inherent in the introspection process he should carefully review the total departmental training needs with an orientation of determining the basis of the needs. In other words, the training needs of command level personnel may cause problems to appear throughout the organization down to the operational level. The most difficult training needs to be determined are those at the administrative level. The chief administrator must have the honesty and integrity to recognize those areas in which he is deficient and have the courage to take the action necessary to correct the deficiencies.

The establishment of a priority among the training needs is the next process in training program development. This priority among the training needs is essential so that those deficiencies requiring immediate correction receive the appropriate attention. While it is to be expected that the opinions of supervisory personnel will be sought during this process, to ensure their continued interest and involvement, command level personnel should be directly involved in the fixing of priorities since their opinions will influence the administrative head who has the final authority. These recommendations concerning priorities should be submitted to the administrative head in the form of completed staff work, and the administrative head should never lose sight of the fact that the final decision rests with him.

Once this priority among the training needs has been established, the next phase in the process is the development of the specific training programs to meet the identified training needs. This phase of the process is one of the prime responsibilities of the departmental training officer, with final program approval resting with the administrative head of the organization. This is not to say the opinions of command and supervisory personnel will not be sought during this phase, but their involvement in this phase is indirect rather than direct.

Command and supervisory personnel are involved in the next phase of the training process, the actual presentation of the newly devised training program, to varying degrees. In some instances personnel at both levels will be involved as instructors, while at other times they may be involved as students. Platoon or shift level training and coach-pupil training provide both command level, to a limited degree, and supervisory level personnel with responsibilities of coordination and administration. Even though the degree of involvement in this phase varies as the training programs vary, there is still a need for the involvement of command and supervisory level personnel. Remember if departmental personnel are to function effectively in the instructor's role, then they must be allotted sufficient time in which to prepare to assume the role.

The final phase of the training process, the evaluation of the training program, will directly involve both command and supervisory level personnel. As part of the evaluation process these personnel should be required to rate or evaluate their subordinates' performance after they have received the training. These evaluations of employee performance must be made in terms of the goals or objectives of the training program. For example: if the objective of a particular training program was to enable patrol officers to be able to satisfactorily operate the 35mm camera, then the evaluation of the training program should be in terms of whether or not the patrol officers can so operate the 35mm camera. In this most critical phase of the training process it is of the utmost importance that the personnel completing the evaluations understand the significance of their evaluations since they will be the primary method whereby the training effort is to be evaluated.

Two factors, involvement and support, have been mentioned when discussing the responsibilities of command and supervisory level personnel. So far little has been mentioned relating to how these personnel can support the training function. Perhaps the best indication these personnel can manifest to display support for the training function is to become *willingly* involved in it. Through this willful involvement in the training function they are indicating they believe in the training programs and they support its goals or objectives.

This chapter has been concerned with the responsibilities of management level personnel to the training function within a police organization. As a result of the proper acceptance of these responsibilities, the organization will benefit in that its employees will be able to perform more effectively because their skills in performing their assigned tasks will be improved and refined. In addition, the attitudes and habits of employees can be changed and shaped to coincide with the goals or objectives of law enforcement. The final benefit to the organization rests in the fact that the turnover of departmental personnel will probably be decreased through the proper application of the training process because of increased job satisfaction.

In summary, the responsibilities of those at the management level within the police organization to the training function are listed as follows:

### CHIEF ADMINISTRATOR

1. To recognize the ultimate responsibility for training rests with the chief administrator.
2. To recognize his responsibility is twofold; to the general public, and to the police organization.
3. To ensure his organization is fulfilling the public's expectations concerning law enforcement.
4. To convince the administrative officers of local government that the training function is worthwhile and deserving of their support.
5. To determine the public's expectations concerning the roles and functions of his organization within the community.
6. To determine public opinion as to how the police organization might be improved.
7. To improve both individual and group performance within the organization by the proper application of the training process.
8. To ensure subordinates are properly oriented toward law enforcement in general, and in particular, his department's role within the community.
9. To develop within subordinates a favorable attitude toward the training function.
10. To recognize the legitimacy of the training function and to support it.
11. To encourage the support and involvement of all organizational personnel, particularly command and supervisory level personnel, in the training function.
12. To ensure the skills and knowledge gained as a result of training are used to benefit the entire organization.
13. To insure the training function within the organization receives the financial support necessary to its success.
14. To ensure the necessary facilities and equipment required to support the training function are available as needed.
15. To select a departmental training officer and to delegate to him the appropriate responsibility and authority.
16. To ensure sufficient time is allotted in conjunction with training program development, presentation and evaluation.
17. To approve training need priorities and the training programs developed to meet these needs.

### COMMAND AND SUPERVISORY

1. To recognize their responsibility is twofold; to the general public, and to the police organization itself.
2. To support the training function within the organization.
3. To become willingly involved in departmental training programs.
4. To become involved in the training need-determination process.
5. To determine the specific training needs of subordinate personnel.
6. To assist in the establishment of the priorities among the identified training needs.
7. To ensure subordinate personnel are performing to the fullest extent of their abilities.
8. To assist in developing the actual training programs to meet or satisfy the identified training needs.
9. To act as an instructor during the presentation of training programs whenever necessary.
10. To actively participate in the training program evaluation process.

*Chapter III*

# THE TRAINING OFFICER: SELECTION, RESPONSIBILITIES AND DUTIES

As previously mentioned, the selection of an individual from within the organization to serve as the departmental training officer is a major responsibility of those at the management levels of the police organization. The final selection should be the sole responsibility of the administrative head of the organization based upon the recommendations of other management personnel. If those at the highest administrative and management levels are to properly fulfil their responsibilities to the general public and the organization, then someone within the organization must be responsible for the training function.

Since the role of the training officer is a specialized function, the administrative head may want to consider the possible lateral entry of qualified outside personnel to fill the position. While this is an excellent method whereby the position may be filled by a qualified individual, the administrator of the smaller police department may not choose this option. In fact, in smaller police organizations the entire process of seeking qualified outside personnel may well be an unnecessary expense. Usually, it will be extremely difficult for a small police organization to offer a salary sufficient to attract outside personnel.

While the training needs of larger police organizations will require the services of a training officer on a full-time basis, such will not usually be the case where smaller organizations are concerned. The exception is that instance where the organization's involvement in the training function has been practically nil and there is a need to get the expanded training program *off the ground.* When the training officer assignment is to be made on a part-time basis, they are commonly referred to as *zebra* assignments. Simply speaking, an assignment of this nature means the

23

individual so assigned as the departmental training officer will have other responsibilities in addition to being responsible for departmental training efforts. In many instances the initial assignment will of necessity have to be on a full-time basis which, once training programs have been established, can become a part-time assignment. In this regard the administrator will have to *play it by ear* as to when to make the change from full-time to part-time. This is not to say a cutoff date can not be established, but the administrative head will have to decide when this stage of development is reached. Perhaps during the need-determination phase of the process it would be more advantageous to select a committee to determine the departmental training needs, and to recommend a priority among them, before turning the job over to an individual on a full-time basis. Once the training needs have been identified and a priority among them established, the training officer can devote all his attention to developing specific training programs to meet the needs.

Even though the assignment as departmental training officer is made on a part-time basis, it is necessary to ensure adequate time is allotted to the training officer for the satisfactory completion of the training related tasks. In addition, it is important to realize if departmental training has been somewhat in limbo due to the lack of someone being designated as being responsible, the initial phase of the operation will require large amounts of time in order to determine the training needs of the organization and to develop the training programs to meet these needs.

When considering the individuals within the organization for the position of departmental training officer, all members of the organization should be reviewed as possible candidates; however, those at the command and supervisory levels will generally be the most qualified by virtue of their experience, exposure to the organization, training received and position within the organization. The following considerations should be taken into account when reviewing candidates for the position, whether or not they come from within the organization:

1. The candidate should have an interest in the training function and its relationship within the police organization. This may be demonstrated by the candidate functioning as the departmental

training officer on an informal basis or by a desire on his part to improve himself through individual effort.

2. The candidate should be aware of how the training function fits into the police organization and of training's responsibilities to both the general public and the police organization.

3. The candidate should be willing to devote the extra time and effort required to ensure the training function is meeting its responsibilities to the general public and the organization.

4. The candidate should possess, or have the ability to learn, the skills and knowledge required to perform the administrative tasks which are an integral part of the training function such as planning, reviewing, budgeting, scheduling, researching and evaluating.

5. The candidate should be aware of the various types of training programs that are available and of the types of outside specialized training that is available.

6. The candidate should be aware of the various training methods that may be employed within the police organization, and the circumstances under which they may be best used.

7. The candidate should be capable of accepting the responsibility of the position and of selling the training function to other members of the organization.

8. The candidate should be aware of the various forms of assistance that are available to assist in the development or improvement of the departmental training function.

9. The candidate should be aware of the nature and scope of the organization's involvement in training in the past and what the future plans concerning training encompass.

The most important of these considerations is that the candidate have a real or genuine interest in police training and the desire to improve training within the organization. Making a decision in this regard obviously requires a value judgement on the part of the administrative head of the organization; however, the past performance of the candidates can provide information concerning this area. If the interest in training is present within the individual and the organization is willing to assist, then the other desired attributes can probably be developed within the individual.

In addition, the candidate should be questioned as to what he feels should be the direction and goals of the training programs within the organization. The candidate should have some general goals or objectives in mind and some views as to how these goals or objectives might best be achieved. In this same vein he should have an understanding of the goals and objectives of training as viewed by the administrative head.

The final selection of the training officer should be made by the administrative head of the organization after receiving the recommendations of command and supervisory personnel and after reviewing each candidates qualifications. Command and supervisory personnel should only submit recommendations concerning candidates who are subordinate to them within the organization or who are from outside the organization. All members of the organization should be made aware of the fact that a training officer is being sought, and if they are qualified for or interested in the position, they should make their desires known to the administrative head in writing. Even at this early stage in the development of the departmental training function it is important to demonstrate training involves everyone within the organization and their individual involvement is sought. In addition, once the selection is made, the training officer should use the talents of those who expressed an interest in the position in such phases of the training process as need-determination or program development to maintain their interest and involvement. Remember, half a loaf is better than no loaf at all.

As with any position of responsibility within an organization, it is necessary that the training officer be given the authority commensurate with his responsibilities. Since the role of the training officer is of a staff nature, he should have no responsibility or authority over line operations unless his assignment is of a *zebra* nature or certain emergency conditions arise. Naturally, the extent of his authority will depend upon the nature of his responsibilities. It is sufficient to state at a minimum, the training officer must have the authority to carry out the responsibilities listed below. The duties and responsibilities of the training officer can be broken down into five general areas of activity:

1. Determining the actual training needs at *all* levels within the organization and establishing a priority among these identified needs.
2. Planning the specific training programs to fulfil the identified training needs.

3. Conducting and supervising the presentation of all departmental training programs.
4. Evaluating all departmental training programs once they have been completed to determine their effectiveness.
5. Coordinating all the training activities of the organization into a meaningful whole.

The initial and perhaps most critical operation facing the newly appointed training officer is the need-determination process. No legitimate purposeful training can take place until the training needs of the organization have been identified and a priority among the needs established. (Since the actual need-determination process is explained in detail in the next chapter, it will not be discussed here.) While most of the identifiable training needs of the organization will rest within operational level employees, it is important to recognize the need for additional training will also exist at the supervisory, command and administrative levels. At these levels within the organization it is important that the involved personnel view their need for additional training as an opportunity for self-improvement or self-development rather than as a criticism of their abilities.

Once the training needs of the organization have been established or identified, it is necessary to establish a priority among the needs. This phase of the operation is necessary so that the critical needs receive immediate attention of a corrective nature. The establishment of a priority among the training needs is also a step assuring there will be a logical sequence to the training programs. For example: if the training need-determination process reveals the overall quality of investigations is lacking, then it is only logical to offer training concerned with the preliminary investigation process initially to be followed by a training program concerned with the aspects of the follow-up investigation process. This priority among the training needs must be viewed in terms of not only who needs what type of training now, but also what types of training can the organization best afford in terms of time and money to give now. In addition, the future role of the organization should be considered when establishing this priority so that future training needs are not neglected. Finally, the establishment of this priority among the training needs should be the end product of the joint efforts of the training officer and the administrative head of the organization with inputs from others as deemed appropriate.

Once this priority among the training needs has been established, the training officer has the responsibility of developing the training programs to meet these needs. The first step in program development is to set the goals or objectives for each training program to be undertaken. These goals or objectives must be stated in terms of expected student behaviors rather than instructor behaviors. In other words, the goals or objectives of the training program should clearly state what the students will be able to do, after completing the training program, that they could not do prior to receiving the training. One of the most frequent mistakes made in this respect is to set unrealistic goals or objectives in terms of the time allotted for the training effort. If, for example, eight hours have been allotted in which to conduct firearms training at the basic level, it would be unrealistic to set as a goal the training of the students to be expert classification shooters. It is of the utmost importance that the goals or objectives be ones that can reasonably be attained as a result of the training program. Since the goals or objectives you set for the training program are the primary yardsticks by which you measure the effectiveness of the training program, they must be realistic.

In addition to setting realistic goals or objectives for the entire training program, goals or objectives must be established for the individual units of instruction that comprise the entire training program. As before, the goals or objectives must be stated in terms of student behavior, not instructor behavior. The idea is not to specify what the instructor is to do in the classroom, but to specify what the student is to learn during the instructional period. For example: if the unit of instruction dealt with the Introduction and Nomenclature of the Revolver, Caliber .38 Special, the objectives for the unit of instruction might appear as follows:

Upon completing this unit of instruction the student will be able to:
1. Complete statements on the general characteristics of the caliber .38 revolver.
2. List four safety features in the caliber .38 revolver.

3. Complete statements on safety precautions to be observed before and during disassembly.
4. List the two major assemblies of the caliber .38 revolver.
5. State the part that holds the yoke of the cylinder group to the frame.
6. Given an illustration of the .38 revolver disassembled, match the parts with their proper nomenclature.

As one can readily observe, not only are these objectives stated strictly in terms of student behavior, but they also indicate to the instructor what he is going to have to teach during the instruction period. Once again, these goals or objectives must be realistic in terms of available time so that the effectiveness of the training program may be properly evaluated. The training officer should review and discuss the objectives of the units of instruction with the individual instructors. These review and discussion sessions ensure the instructors are aware of their teaching responsibilities within the allotted time and they can set up their lesson plans accordingly. In addition, these sessions afford the training officer an opportunity to explain how each unit of instruction relates to the others and how they all contribute to the overall objectives of the training program.

In planning training programs to meet the specific training needs the training officer should use as many *qualified* departmental personnel as possible in the role of instructors. This not only adds continuity to the entire program, but it eases some of the difficulties associated with coordinating and scheduling. When subject areas require specialized instructors not available within the organization, arrangements should be made for guest or outside instructors. In some instances the training need may be such that specialized training facilities will have to be used.

Once the training needs have been identified and the priorities established, the steps to be followed in the planning process will be somewhat consistent irrespective of the specific training need to be filled. The steps in the planning process are as follows:

1. Setting the goals or objectives for the training program to be undertaken.
2. Determining what type of training program is to be utilized as the vehicle for training.

3. Determining how many hours of instruction will be required to fulfil the goals or objectives of the training program.
4. Selecting the subject matter that is to comprise the program.
5. Setting the goals or objectives for the individual units of instruction.
6. Scheduling the individual units of instruction within the time allotted for the entire training program.
7. Arranging for the physical facility needs of the program.
8. Estimating the cost of the program.
9. Selecting the personnel to serve as the instructional staff for the program.
10. Arranging for guest or outside instructors when necessary.
11. Selecting the personnel from within the organization to receive the training.
12. Selecting the method of evaluation to be used once the training program has been completed.
13. Presenting the entire program to the administrative head in the form of completed staff work.

The final approval of proposed training programs rests at the highest administrative level of the organization. Through this step the administrator has the final word concerning the nature and extent of the training his personnel receive. It is the function of the training officer to present his proposals concerning training to the administrator in the form of completed staff work.

Once the training program has been approved, personnel scheduled, classes scheduled, etc., the next phase in the operation is the presentation of the program. The training officer has the responsibility of maintaining attendance records, introducing guest instructors, preparing, administering and evaluating examinations and coordinating the overall operation of the program.

Upon completion of the program the training officer has the responsibility of evaluating the program in terms of how well it met the previously determined goals or objectives. Through this evaluation the training officer can measure the effectiveness of the training program and make the necessary adjustments to further upgrade the departmental training efforts. In addition, this evaluation can serve to indicate additional training needs within the organization that have not been previously identified.

The final general responsibility of the training officer is to coordinate the training activities of the entire organization. In this respect specific training programs at the platoon or shift level should complement the general training received at other levels so that there is continuity to the entire program. If individuals have received outside specialized training, what they have learned should be passed on to those within the organization with a similar need. For example: if an officer received specialized training in traffic crash investigation, he would be expected to pass on what he has learned to others within the organization needing additional training in the traffic crash investigation process.

In summary, the duties and responsibilities of the departmental training officer are listed as follows:

1. Determining the actual training needs at *all* levels within the organization and establishing a priority among the needs.
2. Planning the specific training programs to satisfy the identified needs.
3. Conducting and supervising the presentation of all departmental training programs.
4. Evaluating the training programs once they have been completed to determine their effectiveness.
5. Coordinating all the training activities of the organization into a meaningful whole.

*Chapter IV*

☆ ☆ ☆ ☆ ☆ ☆ ☆ ☆ ☆ ☆ ☆ ☆ ☆ ☆ ☆ ☆ ☆

## DETERMINING TRAINING NEEDS

W HILE the legitimacy of the training function is a well recognized responsibility of the organization by many modern police administrators, an untold number of law enforcement administrators still tend to view the training function as a necessary evil. Training within these organizations is generally conducted at minimum levels with little regard for the actual training needs of the individuals or the organization. Any training, whether it be conducted within the organization or outside, must be based upon actual identified training needs of the organization's members at all levels or they will fail. All too frequently training is conducted so that it can be reported to supervising officials. When training simply becomes a method of justifying a larger budget request, without being based upon identified needs, it becomes an exercise in futility.

Even though the management of the police organization has the responsibility to select and support the training programs it becomes involved in, the actual identification of the majority of the training needs can best be accomplished by the first line supervisor. By the first line supervisor we mean the individuals, irrespective of rank, who are directly responsible for the manner in which operational level officers, patrolmen, discharge their duties and responsibilities. In other words, the platoon, shift, watch or section commander is in a position to observe and evaluate the activities of those at the operational level and can assess the impact of administrative level practices and policies upon the rest of the organization. In this respect it is important to recognize those needs identified by the first line supervisor will generally relate to operational level activities such as report writing, traffic crash investigation, field interview techniques, or felony vehicle stop procedures to mention a few. Symptoms indicating training

32

needs in personnel managment, for example at the command and administrative levels, may come to the attention of the first line supervisor; however, he will not usually be in a position to define the training needs at these levels more specifically.

The training needs of the organization are usually discussed in four dimensions. The first of these is the general departmental need. This type of training need relates to either the entire department or a large segment of the department, such as the need for improved intradepartmental communications. A training need of this nature would affect the entire organization, and symptoms of the need would more than likely be apparent at all levels of the organization. In addition, this type of training need would require different types of training programs for the various levels of the organization and should be interrelated.

The second aspect of training needs concerns itself with the general need of a specific group of personnel within the organization. For example: the traffic division may need to improve its reporting procedures. While this type of training need affects the traffic division most directly, it is readily apparent that other elements within the organization, such as records, will also be effected.

The third dimension of the discussion of training needs relates to the specific training need of a specific group of personnel within the organization. As an example: it may be apparent that the supervisory staff of the patrol division has a need for additional training in completing the daily activity summary. This type of training need differs from those previously mentioned in that it is a specific need relating to a specific area, the daily activity summary, rather than a general need such as reporting procedures.

Finally, the scope or depth of the training need of the specific group within the organization must be determined. It is not sufficient to merely state the supervisory staff of the patrol division needs additional training in completing the daily activity summary. The need must be specifically defined so that it is known how much of what kind of training will be required to elevate their performance to a satisfactory level. The second consideration in this particular situation is perhaps obvious, it being how many members of the supervisory staff are actually in need of this training? It may well be that some of the members of the supervisory staff do not need the additional training and to require their attendance at a training session would be a waste of time and resources.

The actual need-identification process is based upon an analysis of the organizational problems and conditions. In conjunction with this analysis, a supplemental analysis of the employee's performance, problems and potential should be conducted. Three techniques may be utilized in conducting these analyses: asking, observing and studying. The entire process must be a cooperative effort of employees, supervisors, management and the training staff.

The initial technique of analysis, asking, relates to all three levels of the organization: operational, supervisory and administrative. Types of questions that should be asked at the management level are:

1. What are the areas in which you believe your department's operations need the most improvement?
2. What tasks should your staff be better able to perform than they do at present?
3. Why should your staff be able to perform these tasks in a more effective manner?
4. What are the effects of present staff weaknesses on departmental programs?
5. What is the size and nature of your need for personnel replacements, present and near future, especially in key administrative, technical and supervisory positions?
6. How will this need for replacement personnel be effected by anticipated program trends, expansion and contraction within the organization?
7. How do you plan to meet this need for replacement personnel within the organization?
8. What staff duties have you undertaken due to the lack of qualified subordinate personnel?
9. To whom and to what extent have you delegated staff duties and responsibilities to subordinates?
10. In what respects has your own level of performance been less than what you would desire?

11. What specific steps have you taken to improve the performance of subordinates?
12. Who within the organization has the overall responsibility for training?

This list of questions is not all-inclusive, but it does indicate the nature of the questions that should be asked of management level employees when attempting to determine training needs. Remember primarily we are seeking to identify organizational training needs, but we should also be seeking to identify specific training needs of management level personnel. Questions of this type tend to focus attention on immediate, already-recognized training needs and less obvious training needs can be identified by less direct questions.

The next level of questioning should take place at the supervisory level, and if properly conducted, can prove most beneficial since the supervisor has a working relationship with both the operational and administrative levels of the organization. During this phase of the questioning there is a tendency to place emphasis upon operational level training needs. This emphasis is desirable, however, not to the exclusion of the individual supervisor's training needs or administrative level training needs. Examples of the types of questions that should be asked of supervisory level personnel are:

1. What are the specific areas in which you most want your subordinates to improve their levels of performance?
2. What are the causes for these substandard levels of performance?
3. How do these substandard levels of performance effect departmental programs?
4. In what areas would you like to have your subordinates develop a proficiency that does not now exist?
5. What specifically have you done to improve the performance levels of your subordinates?
6. In what specific areas do you feel your own training has been deficient?
7. In order to raise performance to a satisfactory level, what type of assistance do you need and from whom?
8. To what extent do you agree with your subordinates' analysis of the problems facing the organization?
9. In what specific respects do you feel the training of superior

personnel has been deficient?

10. How do you determine a subordinate is in need of a specific type of training?
11. What training do you provide your subordinates on a regular basis?

The third level of questioning activity should take place at the operational level of the organization. It is quite likely the bulk of the organization's training needs will rest within the operational level employees, and therefore they should be questioned in detail. Generally speaking, when questioning those at the operational level, it is advisable not to ask them what types of training they think they need. Many operational level employees have not had enough exposure to the law enforcement role to respond in a meaningful manner to questions of this type. They tend to respond in terms of the types of training they personally would like to have rather than what they actually need to improve their performance. This type of training falls into the nice-to-know rather than the need-to-know category. Examples of the types of questions to be asked of those at the operational level are as follows:

1. How do you feel about your job with the department?
2. What do you like most about your job?
3. What do you like least about your job?
4. What part(s) of your job give(s) you the greatest difficulty?
5. How do you feel this difficulty affects you personally?
6. How do you feel this difficulty affects your supervisor?
7. How do you feel this difficulty affects departmental programs?
8. What is the cause of this difficulty?
9. What aspects of your performance do you want to improve the most?
10. What are you personally doing in an attempt to improve your performance?
11. Do you need help from others to improve your performance?
12. What kind of help, from whom, do you need to improve your performance?
13. How has your supervisor assisted you in improving your job performance?
14. Is the department allowing you to develop your abilities to the fullest potential?

15. What specific strengths do you have that the department is not making maximum use of?

All these questions can be helpful in determining training needs; however, use may dictate that in some circumstances the desired information is not being obtained. In these instances the questions should be modified or substitute questions prepared to obtain the desired information. Remember, the objective of the questioning process is to determine the *specific* performance areas in which work levels are substandard and to determine why they are substandard.

The second phase of this analysis to determine departmental training needs involves the observation of the organization in operation. This phase of the analysis should concern itself with merely recording the manner in which the organization operates on a day-to-day basis rather than attempting to identify the *whys* of the operation. This observation of organizational operations should encompass the following areas:

A. *Morale factors*
   1. Does personal friction exist between the various levels of the organization?
   2. Does *buck passing* or the failure to accept responsibility exist among those who should be accepting the responsibility?
   3. Do complaints, either unfounded or based in fact, generate from those involved in supervisory-subordinate relationships?
   4. Is there evidence of inattention to work by members of the organization?
   5. Are there cases where leadership roles have been assumed by those not appointed to positions of leadership?
   6. Are supervisors effective in providing their subordinates with some sense of worth, belonging and security?
   7. Are there indications of a lack of supervisory support of subordinates?
   8. Does there seem to be an absence of a sense of purpose and accomplishment among those within the organization?
B. *Job Knowledge*
   1. What is the level of performance in the technical phases of the operation?
   2. What is the level of performance in the administrative phases of the operation?

3. What is the level of performance in the supervisory phases of the operation?
4. What is the level of performance in the operational phases of the operation?
5. Are employees performing at levels lower than is expected and as a result causing subordinates to carry the load?

C. *Communications*
1. Are written and oral instructions misunderstood or misinterpreted?
2. Is there a failure in information flowing across, up and down within the organization?
3. Are accepted or designated lines of communication being ignored or bypassed for informal lines?
4. Is there an ability, on the part of those required to do so, to express themselves either orally or in writing?
5. Are written communications brought to the attention of all concerned?

D. *Supervision*
1. Are work assignments made in accordance with the abilities of subordinates and overall aims of the organization in mind?
2. Are supervisors planning and scheduling work in accordance with accepted techniques?
3. Are supervisors instructing subordinates in accordance with their needs?
4. Are greviances, both real and imagined, being handled at the supervisory level when appropriate?
5. Is there a lack of job pride on the part of the supervisors and/or their subordinates?
6. Does the supervisor and/or his subordinates display a lack of interest in the job?
7. Does the supervisory staff fail to recognize and motivate subordinates?
8. Is the supervisory staff able to explain the orders and policies generated from administrative level employees?

E. *Job application*
1. Are employees applying the job knowledge and skills they possess in the performance of their jobs?
2. Is there a desire to improve, through self-improvement, one's performance?
3. Are the specialized skills and knowledge of employees used to the maximum benefit of the organization?

The third and last phase of the analysis concerns itself with studying the organization and its operation. This phase differs from the second phase in that it is concerned with identifying the *whys* underlying the problems identified during the observation phase. Areas within the organization where this examination phase of the analysis should take place are:

A. *Organizational plans*
1. Are there any projected changes in the mission of the organization?
2. What is the nature of these anticipated changes in the mission of the organization?
3. Are there any projected changes in the structure or organization of the department?
4. What form can these expected changes in the structure of the organization be expected to take?
5. Are there any projected changes in personnel assignments within the organization?
6. Why are these changes in personnel assignments being made?
7. Are there any projected changes in departmental operating procedure?
8. Who will be affected by these changes in operating procedures?
9. Why are these changes in operating procedure being made?

B. *Employee records*
1. Has the organization been experiencing a higher than normal turnover rate?
2. Is the rate of absenteeism among employees higher than should be expected?
3. Are employees becoming involved in accidents at an abnormal rate?
4. Are greviances being presented at an abnormal rate and generally not based on facts?
5. Do merit ratings reflect the true status of personnel?
6. What is the composition of the operational level employees in terms of length of service, training, education and experience?
7. What is the composition of the supervisory staff in terms of length of service, training, education and experience?
8. What is the composition of administrative level employees in terms of length of service, training, education and experience?

C. *Official inspection reports*
1. Carefully examine both those done by the organization and those prepared by outside agencies.

2. Are those inspections required by the department being conducted in accordance with existing procedures?
3. What aspects of the official inspection reports coincide with the results of the training need-determination analysis?
4. What aspects of the official inspection reports conflict with the results of the training need-determination analysis?
5. What new training needs are reflected in the official inspection reports that were not developed during the training need-determination analysis?

D. *Work and work-flow*

1. Do bottlenecks exist in the currently existing work-flow procedures?
2. What is the nature and cause of these bottlenecks in the existing work-flow procedures?
3. Is work output more or less consistent or do peaks and valleys appear where they should not exist?
4. What is the nature and cause of these variations in the work output of the organization?
5. Do departmental records indicate there are high costs, wasted effort and excessive errors?
6. What is causing these high costs, waste of effort and excessive errors?

E. *Supervisory selection*

1. What type of process exists for the selection of supervisory personnel?
2. Is the supervisory selection process applied consistently irrespective of the personnel involved or candidates for promotion?
3. Are the requirements for supervisory positions such that the most qualified personnel are selected?
4. What types of training do supervisory personnel receive to prepare them to properly assume the supervisory role?

F. *Command officer selection*

1. What type of process exists for the selection of command level personnel?
2. Is the command officer selection process consistent in its application irrespective of the personnel involved or candidates for promotion?
3. Are the requirements for command level positions such that the most qualified personnel are selected?
4. What types of training do command level personnel receive to prepare them to properly assume the role of a command officer?

G. *Records*
  1. Are patrol officers required to submit daily activity reports detailing their patrol activities?
  2. Are supervisory level personnel required to submit daily and monthly activity reports?
  3. Are these daily and monthly activity reports submitted by patrol officers and supervisory personnel gathering the desired information?
  4. Are all departmental records providing the information they were designed to provide?
  5. Is the records system such that the desired information can be readily obtained?

The foregoing represents a limited examination of the methods that may be used in conducting an analysis of the organization and its employees to determine training needs. There are several techniques whereby these methods of analysis may be implemented, one of which is the interview. The use of the interview in the training need-determination process has several advantages. The first of these is that it can reveal the facts as well as the feelings, causes and possible solutions relating to certain problems. It is extremely important, because of the release of feelings and opinions, that a careful distinction be drawn between fact and opinion. The interview, if properly conducted, affords an opportunity for the free interchange of ideas relating to problem areas and potential solutions to these problems.

The interview is limited, however, in that it can make the interviewee feel he is on the spot and therefore reluctant to be open and candid. This disadvantage can be lessened if the interviewer allots time during the initial portion of the interview to establish rapport between himself and the interviewee. In addition, the interviewer should explain the nature and purpose of the interview and should not limit the interview process to a few selected members of the organization. Since the interview process can be quite time-consuming it will probably not be possible to interview everyone within the organization in detail, and this should not really be necessary. Once a series of interviews has established a particular need, there is no reason to reinforce it.

The questions to be used during the interview process should be pretested to ensure the information sought will be obtained. This pretest should be conducted with a small random group within the organization, perhaps with the supervisory staff at a staff meeting, and the defective questions should become readily apparent. In addition, during the actual application of the interview process, the interviewer should be aware of the fact that defects will still probably exist in the process and be prepared to note them.

Finally, the interviewer should make certain during the interview process that he can and does listen to what is being said. He should not sit in judgement, or give the impression that he is, of the responses given and should only ask questions not included in the formal process to clarify responses. Remember the interview process should be used solely to gain information, not to interpret, sell or educate.

The second technique that may be utilized in this analysis to determine training needs is the questionnaire. The questionnaire can be used to reach a relatively large portion of the organization at a relatively low cost. In addition, it gives the opportunity for expression without fear or embarrassment and the resulting data can be easily summarized and reported. It is limited in that there is little provision for free expression unless the responses are designed to be open-ended; time must be taken in the construction of the questions so that the desired material is obtained; and the responses generally reveal the symptoms of a problem rather than identifying causes and possible solutions.

As with the interview, the contents of the questionnaire should be pretested and revised prior to administering the questionnaire. Also, this pretest should be administered to a small random group within the organization. If the questionnaire technique is used, then you must be prepared to report the results, both favorable and unfavorable, and be prepared to take action concerning the unfavorable aspects.

The third technique that may be utilized is job analysis and performance review. This technique can provide specific and precise information concerning job performance since it is directly tied to actual jobs and job performance. Through job analysis the job is broken down into segments manageable both for training and appraisal purposes. This technique is severely limited in that it is very time consuming and difficult for those not adequately trained in job analysis techniques. The job analysis can be used to reveal training needs of the individuals within the organization but not those based on the needs of the organization per se. It is important to ensure the job analysis is based upon a current job description which reflects the current job. In addition, you should be prepared to review with the employees your analysis of the job and your appraisal of his performance. Job analysis and job or performance review is nothing more than breaking the job into measureable elements and then measuring the individual's performance of the various elements against an acceptable level of performance.

This then is the training need-determination process. Training need-determination is essential before any training program can be developed since training must be based upon the actual identified needs within the organization. The training need-determination process must involve all levels of the organization so that priorities may be established and the training programs may be integrated into a meaningful whole. Effective training programs should complement each other and be part of the established activities of the organization.

In summary, the four dimensions of training needs within the organization are identified as follows:

1. The general departmental need.
2. The general need of a specific group within the department.
3. The specific need of a specific group within the department.
4. The scope or depth of the specific need.

The actual training need-identification process is based upon an analysis of the organizational problems and conditions, and the methods to be used in this analysis are:

1. Asking.
2. Observing.
3. Studying.

Several techniques may be used to implement these methods involved in the training need-determination process, and they are:

1. Interview.
2. Questionnaire.
3. Job analysis and performance review.

# Chapter V

# TYPES OF TRAINING PROGRAMS

T HE solution of the various types of problems one encounters during life will require the application of different approaches or solutions to individual problems. This principle holds true when selecting the type of training program to satisfy the specific training needs within the police organization. The type of training program that will be most successful in meeting the training needs at the operational level will not necessarily be successful in meeting the training needs at the supervisory or other levels. The nature of the training need then is the determining factor, to a large extent, when selecting a type of training program. For example: if two individuals at the management level have a need for additional training in a specific area, the type of training program which will best fill this need would not necessarily be used to meet the training needs of recruit level officers.

Another factor to consider when selecting the type of training program to be utilized is the degree to which it will be recognized and supported by those at the administrative level within the organization. Certainly there will be no support for a training program that is not in the best interests of the department and the general public, or that does not meet the identified training need. Without administrative support and recognition the training program is doomed to failure before it starts. As an example: there may be an identified training need at the operational level for additional training in the techniques associated with vehicle stopping and occupant control. There would be no support, either administratively or by the general public, for a training program that advocated the indiscriminate stopping of motorists merely for training purposes.

When considering the type of training program to be used it is a good idea to also consider those training programs already in existance within the organization. It may be possible to meet the current need merely by using a training program that now exists. If the need is of a specific nature, i.e. the proper completion of a traffic summons, and there exists within the organization a roll call training program, it might well be the most appropriate vehicle for this additional training. There is no need to develop special training programs if the proper vehicle exists within the organization.

Another important consideration is the number of competent instructors available to teach in the program. If the training need is of the type that will require instruction in specialized or technical areas, are instructors available? If not then the training need might be better filled by an organization specializing in this type of training. If the need is of the type that will be reoccurring, then perhaps steps should be taken to develop a core of competent instructors within the organization. As an example: there will probably be a need for firearms training at the basic or recruit level and at other levels within the organization to varying degrees. The need for training of this type will quite probably continue to exist as long as the department does. Rather than having to depend upon outside or guest instructors, why not develop your own departmental firearms instructor?

Generally one of the most difficult problems facing the training officer when selecting a training program type is the amount of time available in which to conduct the training. It may seem there is never enough time available in which to conduct the program at what is felt to be a satisfactory level. In situations of this type it is usually best to pare the program to a minimum level which will still permit the attainment of your goals or objectives for the program. This will normally involve making a sharp distinction between that knowledge which is required and that which is nice to know. If the time available is less than the required minimum, then it may be necessary to split the training program into smaller units or to seek the services of outside training organizations. For example: you might feel forty hours of instruction is the absolute minimum required to meet the training need, however, you have only fifteen hours available in which to conduct the training.

Perhaps the best solution would be to use the fifteen hours at the basic or recruit level and fill in the remaining twenty-five hours at the platoon level over an extended period of time.

Another problem that is almost as vexing as the time problem relates to the availability of the proper training facilities. Naturally a training program cannot be conducted unless the required facilities are available, however, it is surprising just how many times the required facilities can be located with a little extra effort. If the department has no classroom or area that can be utilized as such, the required space can usually be found somewhere within the community. Schools, businesses and other community organizations will generally be able to provide the space required and the necessary adjunct equipment such as projectors, screens, chalkboards or other training aids. Other special needs such as firing ranges or driving ranges represent other areas of difficulty but generally can be resolved through community effort. Limited physical facilities will require modifications in the training programs; however, the overall objective, that of conducting the needed training, can be realized.

The selection of a training program type will also be greatly influenced by the funds available for training. If unlimited funds are available for training, then certainly the most ambitious types of training programs could be undertaken. Such is not generally the case in law enforcement today. Great strides have been taken in recent years both at the state and federal levels concerning the funding of law enforcement training and education. The fact remains if your department has limited funds available, then your training programs will have to be modified to fit within the organization's resources. Training costs can be substantially reduced by using departmental facilities and members of the organization as the instructional staff, if they are qualified.

When selecting the type of training program to meet a specific need, the availability of this type of needed training from sources outside the department should be taken into consideration. Having the needed training conducted by facilities of this type will naturally increase training costs; however, there are certain types of training needs that can best be met by outside agencies. While the training costs increase, the quality of the training received should also increase since the outside agencies can devote the appropriate funds and resources to the training effort. In addition, it is wise not to overlook the possibility of having the outside agency come to your department to conduct the needed training.

Some additional factors to be considered when selecting a training program type relate to the objectives or goals of the training program, the group within the organization to be trained and the level of the personnel to receive the training. If the goals or objectives of the training program are concerned with the mastery of a skill or set of skills, then the training program type should include some practice of these skills. If the goals or objectives are related to imparting some specific knowledge, not involving the mastery of skills, then another type of training program will be more appropriate. The other two considerations relate to the past experience, training and education of the group to be trained. In addition, the size of the group that will be receiving the training must be taken into account. The type of training program selected should be the one most suited to attaining the goals or objectives of the program with the other factors being considered.

Many types of training programs can and are being used by law enforcement agencies. Probably the type of training program most frequently encountered is in-service training. Many forms of in-service training are used, however, they all have the same general objective, to improve a present employee's performance or to prepare him for a specific job, irrespective of the form they take. Areas in which in-service training is frequently applied are:

1. Recruit or basic level training.
2. Regularly scheduled refresher or advanced level training.
3. Continuous in-service training.
4. Roll call training.
5. Nonscheduled special in-service training.
6. Training bulletins.
7. Coach-pupil training.
8. Training conferences.
9. Prepromotional training.
10. Supervisory training.
11. Command level training.
12. Administrative level training.

13. Technical training.

As can be seen from this list in-service training can and has been applied at all levels within the police organization. As is the case in determining which type of general training program will best meet the identified training need, there are certain considerations to be made when examining the various types of in-service training.

The first of the in-service training areas to be examined is the recruit or basic level training. The initial factor to consider concerning recruit level training is the size of the organization. If the organization is small in size or the turnover rate low, then it will probably not be in the best interests of the organization to conduct its own recruit or basic level training. In either one of these instances the number of personnel needing the training will probably be small and to conduct an in-service training program would be an expensive proposition. Training at the recruit or basic level in the absence of a formal training program can be accomplished via the coach-pupil method of training which will be examined in detail later in this chapter. In other instances it may be more advantageous to have the required recruit level training conducted by an outside specialized agency.

Another factor to be considered, irrespective of the size of the department, is the availability of an outside specialized agency to conduct the recruit or basic level training. If a specialized agency exists within reasonably close proximity to the department, you might well use the facilities if they meet your needs. This usage will allow more time for the development of additional training programs within the organization that are needed by other departmental personnel. It is wise to remember that personnel being trained by outside specialized agencies will require additional training in those operational areas indigenous to the local department. Such areas requiring additional departmental training would include local ordinances, departmental policy and procedure, procedures for handling evidence, juveniles, completing various departmental forms and reports, and other operating procedures.

The amount of time to be made available for instruction at the basic or recruit level, whether it be by your department or by an outside agency, may be limited. It may be the time limitation is such that adequate time is allotted to each area of instruction; however, if such is not the case there are solutions. Formal training programs can be supplemented via the coach-pupil training method or through other types of training programs. Naturally, the type of supplemental training program to be used will depend upon the nature of the training to be conducted.

The other factors that need to be considered concerning recruit or basic level training are basically the same as those identified in the process of selecting a general training program type. The availability of instructors, facilities and funds all enter into the picture, and modification of the program may be necessary because of limitations in the foregoing areas.

The next area of in-service training mentioned is regularly scheduled or advanced level training. Through training at the basic or recruit level about the most one can realistically hope to accomplish is to start the recruit officer thinking and acting in a desired manner. Regularly scheduled refresher or advanced level training serves to further hone skills and to reinforce attitudes learned during recruit level training. This training should be consistent with what is taught at the recruit level and should in part exist to correct those deficiencies existing in the recruit level training program. It can also serve as the vehicle through which officers are trained in new techniques, policies or procedures.

One of the most important considerations concerning this type of training is when it is to take place; that is, during the officer's off-duty time or on departmental time. If the training is to take place during the officer's off-duty time, then he should be compensated in some manner, whether it be compensatory time off or partial, full-time or time and a half pay. Naturally, if the training takes place on departmental time, i.e. while the officer is on duty, there is no consideration given to compensation, however, the administrator of the department should expect a decrease in services while the training is being conducted. If the training is to be conducted on departmental time then it will be necessary to offer the training program several times to ensure coverage of all involved departmental personnel.

While regularly scheduled refresher training takes place two or three times during the year, continuous in-service training takes place on a more frequent basis. Training of this type usually occurs on a weekly or monthly basis, and all officers involved are required to receive the training. The same question concerning whose time is to be used to conduct the training arises, as does the question of compensation. In most instances training of this type can be conducted during the officer's on duty time. This type of training can be used to correct deficiencies or to explain new policies, procedures or departmental orders. The major difference between regularly scheduled refresher training and continuous in-service training is the scope or depth of the programs. Continuous in-service training, due to its frequency, lacks the depth of coverage found in regularly scheduled refresher training.

Another type of continuous in-service training is applied at the shift or platoon level. To implement this type of training the training officer prepares short, fifteen to twenty minutes, lesson plans or teaching outlines dealing with the selected subject matter. These lesson plans are then given to the shift or platoon commanders who are instructed to conduct the training on an individual basis with their assigned officers. Further, they are instructed that they will be allotted seven to ten days to complete the training topic, depending upon the number of personnel assigned to the shift or platoon, and the individual officer's completion of the topic should be a matter of record. The training officer should keep a master list of all officers and the training they have completed.

Training of this type can best be applied to skill areas such as photography or fingerprinting, however, limited knowledge areas can be approached. Special topics, such as recent changes in the law, can be inserted into the previously defined priority of needs as they arise without any significant interruption in the overall program. The subject matter should be integrated so that one week's topic might deal with fingerprinting persons, the next week's might deal with locating and developing latent fingerprints and the next week's with photographing and lifting developed latent fingerprints. In this manner student or officer interest is more easily maintained, and there is overall continuity to the training program.

Another type of in-service training which closely parallels

continuous in-service training is nonscheduled or special in-service training. Training of this type exists to deal with special problems as they arise in the course of normal day-to-day operations and might concern themselves with such matters as:

1. Anticipated civil disturbances.
   a. Review of existing tactical plans.
   b. Crowd and riot control.
2. Police authority to strike.
3. The emergence of a specific or special need of a specific group within the organization.
4. New processes or procedures involving a large segment of the department that require immediate attention.

Once again the questions of time and compensation arise, but they are further emphasized by the urgency of the need. As with some of the other types of training it may be necessary to conduct the training program several times to ensure complete coverage of the involved personnel.

The next example of in-service training is roll call training. Training of this type takes place at the roll call or briefing period of the various segments or elements in the organization and would under most circumstances take five to fifteen minutes to complete. The material should be prepared by the training officer and distributed to the supervisor of the particular element in the organization whether it be the Detective Bureau, Patrol Division or the Traffic Division. The supervisor can either conduct the training himself or delegate the responsibility to a member of the section. By delegating this responsibility the supervisor can develop confidence and interest in the departmental training programs on the part of his subordinates.

Material to be covered during roll call training will be limited by the time available at roll call but may be used to cover lengthy subject areas if broken down into manageable segments. Training of this type lends itself well to a centralized operation and can be readily adapted to the diversified shifts or special needs of specialized elements of the police operation. For example: the Detective Bureau may need specialized training in the field identification of narcotics. Through roll call training the members of the Detective Bureau could be exposed to the various techniques involved without taking time from other operational elements.

A training device that can and should be used in conjunction with roll call training is the training bulletin. The use of the training bulletin should be restricted to providing information for those concerned. This restriction is necessary because of the limited material that can be covered in the space and time allotted. Subjects of a controversial nature should be avoided in the training bulletin since there is little provision for discussion. As previously mentioned, the use of the training bulletin should be limited to the presentation of needed facts or other information. The training officer should prepare the training bulletin and distribute it to the supervisors of the various elements within the organization. A file of past training bulletins should be maintained by the training officer and each new officer should receive those past training bulletins that are relevant. The training officer should ensure the training bulletins contain *how to do it* information such as the proper handling of evidence within the organization or how to tally the daily activity report.

The next type of in-service training listed is coach-pupil training. Training of this type can be used as a supplement to formal recruit training, as a basis for the entire recruit level training or as a vehicle for advanced level training. The coach-pupil process consists of nothing more than assigning the officer in need of the additional training to a coach who will provide the needed training. The most critical phase of the process is the selection of a suitable coach. Since the coach will serve as the primary instructor for the officer, he should be assigned to the officer until the training program is terminated. Naturally, this aspect of the program necessitates the assignment of an identical work schedule to both the coach and the officer. When considering individuals for assignment as coaches it is advisable to have as detailed background information as possible concerning such matters as:

1. Special interests or hobbies.
2. Educational level.
3. General I.Q. level.
4. The results of psychological testing if available.
5. Any specialized training or advanced training that has been received.

6. Previous performance evaluations.

In addition, it is most important to determine the attitude of the potential coaches toward the training circumstance in general and the coach-pupil program specifically. The coach must have a favorable attitude toward the program and should view his assignment or selection to be a coach as an honor, rather than as just another dirty job to be done.

The training officer should prepare a manual containing the material to be covered by the coach during his instruction in the form of teaching outlines with a suggested reading list to supplement the instruction. A checklist should also be prepared by the training officer and should be used by the coach to record the officer's receiving the instruction and his level of understanding in the various subject areas. The coach should assign a daily topic for discussion and also assign, when appropriate, daily readings in preparation for the discussion. As daily work situations arise, they should be related to the material contained within the manual and elaborated upon.

Prior to the initation of the coach-pupil training program the coach should be given the opportunity to review the training material in the manual. He should be appraised of the overall goals of the individual units of instruction and the overall goal of the training program. In other words, he should be advised as to what level he is expected to develop the officer's proficiency and in what specific areas this proficiency is to be developed. In addition, he should be advised that the rate at which the material is to be presented will primarily depend upon the learning ability of the recruit officer under his direction.

When utilizing this form of training at the recruit level areas requiring specialized instruction, such as first-aid and firearms which perhaps are not within the capabilities of the primary coach, should be delegated to those qualified. During periods requiring this type of instruction the officer should be assigned to the special coach under the same conditions as those existing with the primary coach.

Weekly meetings should be held among the training officer and each coach and his recruit officer to evaluate the training program and the officer's progress within it. Special problems should be identified, discussed and resolved. In addition, the coach and the training officer should prepare weekly examinations to further evaluate the officer's progress within the program.

The next type of in-service training program to be considered is the training conference. It can best be utilized to conduct training at the advanced level, supervisory and management levels. This type of training is limited in that the number of participants is limited to those that can realistically participate in the conference. In utilizing this method of training the instructor merely stimulates, guides and summarizes a discussion among the participants. Training of this type can instill a sense of participation and contribution, stimulate thought and act as source of new information and experience. For example: there may exist a need for improvement in the supervisory-subordinate relationships within the organization. Through training of this type the entire supervisory staff would have the opportunity to share experiences and ideas. The objectives of the training conference might be listed as follows:

1. Inspiration.
2. Information.
3. Exchange of information.
4. Training.
5. Problem solving.

Prepromotional training is the next type of in-service training listed, and it plays an important role in the supervisory selection process. Prepromotional training does not exist to teach the candidates the content of the promotional examinations but is preparatory training for those aspiring to assume the supervisory role. Training of this type should be offered by the department to those individuals qualified for the positions. The training should take place in reasonably close proximity to the actual promotional process and define the duties and responsibilities of the supervisory rank being sought. Once again the time question arises, officer's off-duty time or departmental time. If possible the training should take place on departmental time; however, there should be little reluctance on the part of the potential supervisors to donate their time for their self improvement and possible advancement.

In conjunction with prepromotional training the next type of in-service training that enters into the picture is supervisory training. Supervisory training should take place at two general levels: basic training for those entering into the supervisory ranks, and advanced training for those individuals already holding supervisory positions. Generally speaking, the training for the new supervisor should tell him how to perform the job of supervision and should be directed toward telling the established supervisor why he needs to do the job in a particular manner. In many departments, and particularly smaller police organizations, the feeling is that the mere attainment of the supervisory position and the attachment of the appropriate insignia to the uniform makes one a supervisor. Nothing could be further from the truth. The transition from officer to supervisor and the satisfactory functioning in the supervisory role is one of the most difficult adjustments facing today's law enforcement officer.

Supervisory training reinforces prepromotional training in that it also concerns itself with the duties and responsibilities of the position. In addition, those policies and procedures which now more directly effect the supervisor should be explained in detail. The training program should also relate to the current problems that exist within the organization, whether they be morale, pay, benefits or working conditions and how they effect the supervisory staff as well as internal supervisory problems.

A quote from the President's Commission on Law Enforcement and Administration of Justice best summarizes the need for supervisory and management level training:

> An officer is not qualified to administer the complex affairs of a department or to supervise the performance of others simply on the strength of police experience acquired in subordinate positions. Supervisory and middle management personnel perform functions and have responsibilities largely unrelated to their early experience within the agency. Additional skills needed by prospective administrators and supervisors must be acquired through advanced education and specialized training.*

The same basic considerations influencing supervisory level

---

*Task Force Report: The Police, The President's Commission on Law Enforcement and Administration of Justice, U.S. Government Printing Office, Washington D.C., 1967, p. 140.

training affect command and administrative level training. Within smaller police organizations the number of involved personnel may be rather small due to the organizational structure. In instances of this type the training might best be undertaken by an outside training agency or by having them come to the department to conduct the needed training.

Training at the management or supervisory and administrative levels can take several forms depending upon the goal or objective of the particular training program. Some of the training methods that may be employed to meet the varying training needs of those at the command and administrative levels are:

1. Lecture — A formal presentation which best serves as an information giving device. Normally student participation is quite limited.
2. Lecture forum — A lecture presentation followed by a discussion and question and answer period.
3. Symposium — Three or more persons with differing views on a controversial question make a presentation followed by a discussion and question and answer period.
4. Panel discussion — Several persons, knowledgeable in the subject area, discuss the problem before the class.
5. Conference — The gathering of people or students for a period of time to discuss and work with a problem. Some solutions should arise as a result of the conference.
6. Seminar — The students meet under the supervision of the instructor for the purpose of learning through research, discussion and presentation.
7. Workshop — A project oriented learning situation. Small groups of students work with the objective of coming up with a solution, or an approach to a solution, to a previously defined problem.
8. Discussion group — The examination and discussion of a agreed upon topic by the students under the guidance of the instructor.
9. Staff meetings — Meetings among the departmental staff with a prepared agenda involving individual or group solutions, total group discussion and decision making.

As previously mentioned, the actual training needs of those at the command and administrative levels will determine the most appropriate training method to be used.

Another form of in-service training relates to those technical skills that are integral to the police operation. The particular technical skills to which attention should be directed are:

1. Dispatcher.
2. Business machine operator.
3. Identification work, photography, fingerprints.
4. Criminal investigations.
5. Vice control.
6. Traffic control.
7. Traffic crash investigation.
8. Chemical testing for intoxication.
9. Polygraph operators.

In many instances the training needs arising from these technical skills can be met through the coach-pupil method of instruction. Other areas will require the services of an outside specialized agency. Irrespective of the type of training program that is to be utilized, the end result is a core group of trained personnel who can be used to instruct others within the organization with a similar need.

In summary, when selecting a training program type several factors need to be considered:

1. The nature of the training need.
2. The extent to which the training program selected will be recognized and supported by those at the administrative level within the organization.
3. The types of training programs already in existence within the organization.
4. The number of competent instructors available to teach.
5. The time available in which to conduct the training program.
6. The availability of proper training facilities and the required support equipment.
7. The funds available for training.
8. The availability of receiving the needed training from an outside specialized agency.
9. The objectives or goals of the training program.
10. The group within the organization which is to receive the training.
11. The level, educational and experience, of the personnel who will receive the training.

Many types of training programs exist, however, since the scope of this text is limited primarily to training within the department, only in-service training programs have been identified. Many types of in-service training are available, and they are listed as follows:

1. Recruit or basic level training.
2. Regularly scheduled refresher or advanced level training.
3. Continuous in-service training.
4. Nonscheduled special in-service training.
5. Roll call training.
6. Training bulletins.
7. Coach-pupil training.
8. Training conferences.
9. Pre-promotional training.
10. Supervisory level training.
11. Command level training.
12. Administrative level training.
13. Technical training.

☆ ☆ ☆ ☆ ☆ ☆ ☆ ☆ ☆ ☆ ☆ ☆ ☆ ☆ ☆ ☆ ☆

# Chapter VI

# METHODS OF INSTRUCTION

$A$N integral part of any training program is the various methods of instruction used to present the program. Some types of training programs will dictate the use of a particular method of instruction, however, most will be characterized by the usage of several different methods of instruction. A method of instruction is defined as the pattern of instructional activity which is characteristic of the lesson or unit of instruction as a whole. In simpler terms, when discussing methods of instruction one is really discussing nothing more than teaching methods.

It is to be expected, as part of the training officer's role, that the training officer will on occasion be called upon to assume the role of a teacher or instructor. The preparation of training bulletins or the preparation of a manual for coach-pupil training will require the assumption of the teaching role if the material is to serve its intended purpose. Also, if the training officer is to assist others within the organization in assuming the teaching role or in developing their proficiency as teachers, then he must have a complete awareness of the teaching role. Finally, it is only natural for the training officer to insert himself into departmental training programs in the teaching role. Involvement of this nature not only displays his support and interest in the training programs, but also enables him to exercise a degree of control over the program itself.

Before attempting to teach or correctly apply the various methods of instruction it is important to understand how people learn, whether they be police officers or not. This is important because it is safe to say unless learning has taken place, there has been no teaching. Learning is the end product of teaching and has to be the criterion whereby the success or failure of the teaching act is measured. The most common way in which people learn is through the use of the five senses: seeing, hearing, smelling, touching and tasting. One or more of the senses is in constant operation and literally provides us with most of what we learn. It stands to reason the more senses we can appeal to or reach during the teaching process, the more effective the teaching will be in terms of learning. If we view the senses as receptacles into which we can plug our teaching, then that method of instruction which appeals to the majority of the senses has the best chance of being successful.

Perhaps the second most common method whereby people learn is through organized instruction such as is presented in organized departmental training. Obviously if organized instruction is to be effective, then the most effective methods of instruction must be utilized to present the subject matter. In the same regard people also learn through organized purposeful discussion such as planned meetings or conferences. In these instances people usually profit most through the free exchange of ideas and concepts even though the discussion may be somewhat structured.

One of the oldest ways in which people learn is through experience or the *school of hard knocks.* Unfortunately, some people must undergo the same experience several times before they are able to learn or profit from it. Experience learning does play a significant role in the teaching-learning process. It provides the basis whereby the successful teacher is able to relate new or different concepts to previous experiences.

Objective reading is another manner in which people learn — that is also significant to the teacher. Objective reading provides a reference to which new ideas may be attached and can be used to expand upon ideas presented in the classroom. Objective reading is an area from which most everyone can profit if they can be encouraged to read. Other ways in which people learn include experimenting, similar to the school of hard knocks only with more direction, and asking questions. Both have a relationship to the teaching role, however, questioning is of more significance. In any learning situation the levels of learning among the students will vary because of their own capabilities, and the questioning process is one of the best ways to equalize learning and to clarify misconceptions.

The final manner in which people learn is one the successful teacher can never afford to forget. Through teaching others one can learn quite a bit concerning his own limitations and abilities. Every time a teacher finishes a session he should have learned something as a result. Not only can the teacher learn more about himself, but he can also learn more about his students. The learning process occurs on a daily basis and continues until death. The teacher who realizes this has taken the first step toward becoming a successful teacher.

Before beginning the teaching process one must realize certain skills are necessary prequisites to successful teaching. The first of these is a knowledge of the subject matter to be presented. None of us can expect to have a knowledge of all things, therefore, the potential instructor must realize it will be necessary to research a subject area before attempting to teach it. This research should be limited to the scope of the presentation as defined by the unit objective, and the teacher should not expect to be able to provide answers to all questions.

In addition to a knowledge of the subject area, the teacher must have the physical skills required to do the job. Few are born with the natural abilities to automatically become a successful teacher. Those who are successful teachers have learned to be so or have taught themselves. The proper use of voice or gestures or the application of proven techniques is learned behavior which most of us can master.

Finally, the teacher must have the skill to combine his knowledge of the subject matter with the physical skills he possesses into a learning situation. Most of us have probably experienced the situation where we encountered a teacher who had a mastery of the subject matter but was unable to achieve learning because he had not mastered the other skills involved in the teaching process. Conversely, if the teacher has mastered the necessary physical skills, he can make a presentation interesting or entertaining, but unless hc has a knowledge of the subject matter little or none of the intended learning will take place.

Basically there are four methods of instruction the teacher may utilize in the teaching-learning situation and they are:

1. Lecture.

2. Illustrated lecture.
3. Discussion.
4. Demonstration-performance.

Each of these methods will be examined in detail later, but for the moment let us consider some of the factors to be considered in selecting a particular method of instruction. The first and most important factor to consider is the subject matter to be presented. The method of instruction selected should be one that maximizes the potential for learning the subject. For example: if the subject matter to be taught is first-aid, then there is a need for the learning of physical skills. One could select the lecture method of instruction to present the material, however, if skills are to be properly mastered, then the student should be given the opportunity to practice the skills so that proficiency may be developed. Obviously, the demonstration-performance method of instruction, in combination with the lecture or illustrated lecture methods, would be the most effective approach.

The next factors to be considered are the instructor's own personality and abilities. This obviously calls for introspection and honesty on the part of the instructor if he is to be effective. In this self-evaluation the instructor should select the method of instruction that maximizes his assets and minimizes his liabilities. If, for example, the instructor has a deficiency in his speaking abilities and acknowledges it, he will select that method of instruction, such as demonstration-performance or discussion, that minimizes the need for his speaking.

Next, the instructor should consider the educational and experience level of the students who are to receive the instruction. For example: Do they have the background to be able to grasp abstract ideas and manipulate them according to varying situations? Do they have sufficient knowledge of the subject matter to be able to participate in a meaningful discussion? Are the students ignorant of the subject matter so that the presentation should be of an introductory nature? Questions of this nature must be answered before selecting a method of instruction if the selection is to be appropriate.

Another consideration that will influence the selection of a method of instruction relates to the availability of materials. If audiovisual equipment is not available, then it will be extremely difficult to use the illustrated lecture method. The demonstration-performance method can require many types of adjunct materials, the unavailability of which will preclude the use of this method. Remember, check the resources of the local community before eliminating one of these methods of instruction because of a lack of needed materials.

Finally, physical factors, such as class size or classroom size, will influence the selection of a method of instruction. Large classes will almost automatically exclude all methods except the lecture and illustrated lecture. If classroom space is limited, then it may be impossible to use the demonstration-performance method because of the work station requirement. Once again, don't forget the resources of the community.

By far the most frequently used method of instruction is the lecture. In spite of its wide use and acceptance it is one of the most difficult methods whereby one attempts to achieve learning. In spite of its limitations the lecture method can be used in several ways to achieve meaningful learning. One of the initial steps in the teaching process is a statement of goals or objectives for the instruction that is to follow. This statement of goals or objectives should reflect what the student will be able to do or will know upon completion of the unit of instruction. The lecture method affords an excellent technique whereby the students can become aware of these goals or objectives.

Another purpose of the initial phase of the instruction is to create interest among the students in the subject matter and to stimulate their thought processes concerning the subject matter. Once again the lecture method can provide the vehicle to stimulate interest and thought. In addition, the lecture method can be used to impart information on almost any subject. In particular, it can be used to provide introductory material for the remainder of the presentation.

The lecture method is characterized by the fact that its success as a presentation depends primarily upon the abilities of the instructor. As the instructor goes, so goes the lecture. This fact is of the utmost importance when considering the use of the lecture method of instruction. Also, when using the lecture method, there is no restriction upon the size of the group that can receive the instruction. As long as the students can hear and see the instructor, the lecture method can be used.

The limitations or disadvantages connected with the use of the lecture method are sufficient in number to limit its use. The greatest disadvantage to the use of the lecture method is that it really only appeals to one of the five senses, hearing. Should the student decide to *tune out* the presentation then learning will not be achieved. Unless the teacher has a dynamic, interesting personality, an attention-getting method of delivery and a good grasp of the subject matter, the presentation will be limited in its effectiveness. The lecture method also makes it difficult for the teacher to obtain feedback concerning the presentation. It is hard to evaluate the nature and extent of learning achieved when student participation is limited.

When considering the advantages of the lecture method the first that comes to mind is that it is economical. With the lecture method large amounts of information may be presented to large groups at a relatively low cost per student. Also the lecture method affords an excellent way in which to summarize the material covered in the presentation and to stimulate further interest and thinking on the part of the students.

In preparing to teach using the lecture method, or any of the other methods, the initial step is to establish the goals or objectives for the unit of instruction. Once the goals or objectives have been established it will be necessary to research the subject area to gather the required teaching material. The nature or scope of the goals or objectives should guide and limit the depth of the research and particular emphasis should be given to new trends or developments in the field. After the research has been completed the material should be formed into a lesson plan that will guide the instructor during his presentation. Having completed the lesson plan, the teacher should rehearse the entire presentation. This rehearsal should take place before a live audience, wife, friends or fellow teachers, if at all possible. If this is not possible, then a tape recorder or similar device should be used so that some preliminary feedback can be obtained. Not only will this rehearsal allow the teacher to establish time lines for the presentation, but it will also reveal some of the deficiencies in the presentation as structured. Any deficiencies revealed during the rehearsal should be corrected prior to presenting the material to the students.

After all this preparation the crucial test, the actual classroom presentation, takes place. During the classroom presentation the teacher should take care to note student reaction and behavior to the presentation. This is an extremely important aspect of the teaching process because it provides the basis for the final process, the evaluation of the presentation. Having completed the instruction the teacher should review what happened in the classroom and determine whether or not he attained the objectives of the instructional period. If he failed to do so, then some changes will have to be made in the presentation. Even though the objectives may have been attained, there will probably exist some areas in which improvement can be made to further enhance the presentation.

In presenting material via the lecture method of instruction there are four general steps involved:

1. Introduce the lesson. A precise statement of the goals or objectives for the unit of instruction is absolutely necessary. Suggest the students take notes.
2. Present the material to be covered in the lesson in a step by step sequence.
3. Repeat and emphasize the main points to ensure they are being understood by the class.
4. Summarize the lesson.

Since the success of the lecture method primarily rests with the teacher, there are several tips he can utilize to enhance the learning situation:

1. Suggest the students take notes.
2. Define and explain any terminology that may be unfamiliar to the students. Remember these unknown or confusing terms can vary from class to class.
3. Use humor only to develop or emphasize a point. The excessive use of humor can distract from the goals or objectives of the unit of instruction.
4. Change the pace of the presentation to lend variety. Be active and dynamic in your actions.
5. Attempt to pace the presentation to the abilities of the average

member of the class.
6. Ask questions frequently throughout the presentation to ensure learning has been taking place.
7. Encourage the students to ask questions whenever they fail to understand any portion of the presentation.
8. If the unit of instruction is longer than one hour in length, frequently summarize the material.

The second method of instruction is the illustrated lecture. The illustrated lecture is actually nothing more than a combination of the lecture method and the appropriate illustrations, in the form of audiovisual aids, to clarify major or difficult points made during the presentation. The same techniques that are involved in using the lecture method are used with the illustrated lecture with the difference being that visual aids are used. The procedures involved in preparing to use the illustrated lecture method are identical to those used with the lecture method with the exception that the appropriate visual aids must be selected and logically inserted into the lesson plan.

The most obvious advantage in using the illustrated lecture instead of the lecture is that more than one learning sense is utilized. Now not only can the student hear what is being presented, but he can also see visual representations. Remember, the more of the learning senses we can appeal to during the teaching-learning process the greater the likelihood of meaningful learning. In addition, the use of visual aids to explain difficult concepts or ideas can reduce or eliminate the possibility of incorrect mental pictures in the minds of the students. In this respect the illustrated lecture can aid where word pictures are not sufficiently clear to ensure an understanding of a difficult knowledge or skill. For example: imagine how difficult it would be to explain the concept of a correct sight picture without the use of visual aids.

As with the lecture method the success of the illustrated lecture depends primarily upon the instructor. In addition to the tips for the teacher offered in conjunction with the lecture method, the following are offered in conjunction with the illustrated lecture:

1. Make certain all the students can see the visual aid being used.
2. Display the visual aids when they are actually needed. The

excessive use of visual aids can distract from the remainder of the presentation.

3. Use a pointer and the proper techniques for charts, posters, mock-ups and other visual aids.
4. Explain what the visual aid represents in relation to the presentation or the point being made.
5. Don't stand in front of the visual aids.
6. Prior to the presentation check the operation of any audiovisual equipment you plan to use.

The third method of instruction is the directed discussion method. The directed discussion method of instruction involves an instructor-supervised conversation among the students leading to the attainment of the goals or objectives of the unit of instruction. When using this method of instruction it is important that the instructor not dominate the discussion. If the students are to freely discuss and exchange their viewpoints, then the instructor cannot dominate. This is not to say the instructor should not control the discussion in terms of intensity and time since he must if the goals or objectives are to be attained.

The effective use of the directed discussion will require that the instructor have specific information concerning the students who are to take part in the discussion. Unless the students have some knowledge of or experience with the subject matter, they will be unable to take part in the discussion in a meaningful manner. It is not essential that all of the students have the same level of knowledge or experience since those with little knowledge or experience can profit from those who have had a broader exposure.

One of the important general objectives of any method of instruction involves the molding of the appropriate attitudes within the students. The directed discussion is extremely beneficial in molding attitudes since the pressure for change or modification comes from the students' peer group. Students are allowed to express their ideas in their own words, and misconceptions can be cleared up during the discussion. Since the students are forced to express their thoughts, the directed discussion gives the instructor an excellent opportunity to evaluate the students' understanding of material that has previously been presented.

In preparing to teach using the directed discussion method of instruction the instructor should follow the same procedures as outlined for the other methods. When selecting a topic for discussion care should be exercised not to select a topic of a controversial nature such as one man vs. two man patrols. While controversial subjects will probably generate quite a bit of discussion, they do not lend themselves well to an effective discussion because usually no clear-cut conclusions can be drawn.

The lesson plan should be structured to include a sufficient number of thought or response provoking questions or statements. These questions or statements should be of a general nature that do not require factual recall on the part of the students. In addition, the questions should not be of the type that can be answered with a simple yes or no, rather, questions that start with "What do you think . . ." or "What is your opinion . . ." Questions of this type encourage the students to think and then respond. If discussion is to ensue, then these questions should be part of the lesson plan and the instructor should carefully note the responses generated by them so they may be rephrased as needed.

In conducting a directed discussion the initial phase should involve the use of the lecture method to arouse the students' interest, state the goals or objectives, and provide general introductory information concerning the topic to be discussed. Once the necessary introductory information has been presented, the instructor should begin the discussion by asking some of the response provoking questions mentioned previously. Not only should the instructor exercise care not to dominate the discussion, but he should not allow the discussion to be dominated by a few students. Student-to-student exchanges should be encouraged and every student should become involved in the discussion. Quiet students should be drawn into the discussion by the instructor asking directly for their opinion about the topic under discussion.

As points are developed and resolved during the discussion the instructor should restart the discussion with another question or statement. Additionally, as these points are developed and resolved they should be visually listed on the chalkboard and the instructor should frequently summarize the discussion to keep it headed in the right direction. This frequent summary affords the instructor an excellent opportunity to control and direct the discussion toward the desired goals or objectives. Once the students have, through discussion, reached these goals or objectives, the instructor should summarize the entire discussion by restating the major points leading up to the final conclusions and making a restatement of these final conclusions.

The final method of instruction, demonstration-performance, involves the performing of a set of skills by both instructor and students. This method of instruction is the most effective manner in which to develop those skills requiring the manipulation of objects and can be used to teach practically any skill. The techniques to be used will depend upon the size of the class and the nature and complexity of the skills to be learned.

In using the demonstration-performance method of instruction it is extremely important that the presentation follow a logical learning sequence and the students experience early success in the application of the skills. Repeated failures by the students during the initial steps can only lead to frustration which in turn leads to a lack of interest or the impression that they cannot learn this skill. Since this method of instruction has the potential for appealing to a majority of the learning senses, it has the potential for being one of the most successful methods of instruction.

The first step in preparing to teach using the demonstration-performance method of instruction is to complete a job analysis of the skills to be taught. The job analysis consists of specifically identifying the tasks that comprise the job and the skills, knowledge, abilities and responsibilities required of the worker for the successful performance of the job. Once this analysis has been completed the skills, knowledge, abilities and responsibilities must be ordered into the sequence in which they occur in the actual performance of the job. This ordering provides the basic structure for the lesson plan.

Upon completion of the lesson plan the instructor must gather the materials and tools required in performing the job so that each student, or pair of students, will have his own set. As a final step before the presentation the instructor should practice the skills to be taught and compare the procedures involved to those as ordered in the lesson plan. This rehearsal of the skills is extremely important because the more we practice or apply a set of skills the more they become second nature to us. In this process it is possible to overlook critical phases of the operation because of our familiarity with it and the slow step-by-step rehearsal should ensure the inclusion of all phases of the operation.

In presenting the material the instructor should follow a four-step plan:

1. The instructor does the job slowly and carefully. He states *what to do, how to do it,* and the *key points* in the process.
2. The instructor repeats the job at a faster rate, still below the standard speed, and restates *what to do, how to do it,* and the *key points.*
3. The instructor selects an average student to do the job, The student is instructed to state *what to do, how to do it,* and the *key points.*
4. All students practice the job under supervision.

In applying this method of instruction it is advisable to remember effectiveness will fall off if there are more than fifteen students unless the instructor has assistance in the presentation. In addition, the best practice is to have a work station for each student rather than having the students share work stations.

In summary, there are four general methods of instruction the potential instructor may use:

1. Lecture.
2. Illustrated lecture.
3. Directed discussion.
4. Demonstration-performance.

When selecting among these methods of instruction there are five factors the instructor should consider:

1. The subject matter to be presented.
2. The personality and abilities of the instructor.
3. The student level of education, training and experience.
4. The availability of materials.
5. Physical factors.

# Chapter VII

# LESSON PLAN PREPARATION

ONE of the keys to any successful instructional effort is the lesson plan. Some types of training take the form of on-the-spot corrections or instruction, but most instruction of more than several minutes duration should be the result of some preparation on the instructor's part. A lesson plan is an integral part of this process since it provides the instructor with a guide which enables him to make an orderly, logical presentation of the lesson material.

Usually the lesson plan is thought of as some form of written guide, but this is not always the case. If the instruction is to be of short duration, the instructor should take time to prepare a mental lesson plan, or a plan of attack, before presenting the material. This mental process should include a mental review of the subject to be covered to refresh the process in the instructor's mind. In addition, the instructor should consider the potential learner's personality and select the approach that will best achieve the desired result. For example: if a shift or platoon commander observed one of his subordinates was experiencing difficulty in completing a particular form or report, he would want to consider the following factors before attempting to correct the behavior through the use of training:

1. What previous training has the officer received concerning the use of this form?
2. If the officer has received previous training in the completion of the form or report, what form did the training take?
3. Is this the first time the officer has experienced difficulty with this form or report?
4. What is the scope or nature of the problem? Is he experiencing difficulty with the entire form or just certain portions of it?
5. What type of an approach will be best suited to the correction of

this problem?
6. When will be the best time to conduct this training?
7. How long will it take to conduct this training?

With the answers to these questions the shift commander can formulate his lesson plan and proceed accordingly.

Longer or more detailed instructional periods will require the preparation of a written lesson plan if they are to be properly conducted. Ultimately, this lesson plan serves as the outline for conducting the class presentation and enables the instructor to follow through with his carefully made plans to change the behavior of his students in accordance with the goals or objectives of the unit of instruction. The lesson plan keeps pertinent materials and information before the instructor and helps to ensure order and unity to his presentation. In doing so the lesson plan prevents the instructor from getting off the track, omitting essential information and introducing irrelevant ideas and topics.

It must be remembered the lesson plan exists to serve as a guide for the instructor, not as a crutch for him to lean on during the actual presentation. Many of us have probably been exposed to the dull, lifeless presentation wherein the instructor simply read from the lesson plan. The good instructor uses his lesson plan as a reference and does not hold it in his hand. He only reads from his lesson plan when he is quoting statistical information or citing quotations from authorities in the field.

Each instructor should prepare his own lesson plans for each subject he teaches. If the act of teaching is an individual, personal act, then so should be the lesson plans. Once the objectives for the unit of instruction have been determined the preparation of the lesson plan can begin. The first step in lesson plan preparation is to research the subject area to be taught. One of the latent purposes of this research is to provide the instructor with more knowledge about the subject than he will be able to present in the classroom presentation.

The primary purpose of this research is to allow the instructor to gain a mastery of the subject to be taught. Research allows the instructor to obtain basic or elementary information about the subject and to become aware of any recent developments or trends in the field. It should be emphasized this research should not be a one time proposition which is only conducted during the initial preparation of the lesson plan. As we all know, change takes place on an almost constant basis, and the good instructor will never get caught in the classroom with old or outdated material. As a result the research process is of a continuing nature if the instructor is to properly discharge his responsibilities as an instructor.

In addition to providing basic or elementary information about the subject, the research process should also provide the instructor with supplemental information that can be used to expand the presentation. This supplemental information should not only be useful to the student in that it amplifies or clarifies major points made during the presentation, but it should also be interesting to the student. For example: if the subject matter is traffic crash investigation it would be useful to point out approximately 55,000 people die annually as the result of traffic collisions, however it becomes more interesting to the student if this figure is compared to other information such as the total combat deaths during one year of a given war.

During the research process the instructor will normally encounter much more material than he can hope to present during the time period allotted for his instruction. Consequently it becomes mandatory for the instructor to sift through this material to select that which he can best use during his presentation. In doing so the instructor should have one objective in mind, "Will the material help the students to achieve the desired learning outcome?" The desired learning outcomes, objectives, of the unit of instruction should always dictate the type and amount of material to be presented during the instructional period. Usually time restrictions are such that not enough time is available in which to conduct the unit of instruction as desired. Since this is the case, there can be no justification for including material that in no way contributes to the objectives of the instructional unit.

Finally, the research process can provide the instructor with a list of supplemental readings that can further the student's knowledge of the subject area. As previously mentioned, the research process may well develop information that, because of time limitations, cannot be included in the lesson plan. If the instructor feels this information is significant to the student's understanding of the subject matter, it can be included as supplemental reading to take place outside the classroom. In addition, these supplemental readings may be of a voluntary nature in the form of a suggested reading list for those who desire to increase their knowledge of the subject matter.

Once the research process has been completed the instructor must select the framework against which to attach the material that has been gathered. Essentially there exist two types of lesson plans: the topic, or sentence, lesson plan and the manuscript, or narrative, lesson plan. The topic, or sentence, lesson plan usually is composed of several words or a sentence explaining a topic or point within the planned presentation. A lesson plan of this type essentially serves to remind the instructor of the major points to be covered during the class session. In addition, the topic or sentence lesson plan will permit the students to take more meaningful notes since most of us have been trained to take notes following the outline format. Lesson plans of this type tend to ensure the major points in the presentation are covered and recorded by the students.

The largest single disadvantage associated with the use of the topic or sentence lesson plan is that details or supportive information are not included within the lesson plan and therefore must be in the instructor's mind. As such there is a strong likelihood the presentation will vary from time to time since the instructor may not be consistent in the supportive information he calls to mind during a particular unit of instruction. Also, any research the instructor may have completed is lost for future reference not only to himself but to anyone else who might be interested in the subject matter, such as replacement or substitute instructors.

The second type of lesson plan, the manuscript, or narrative type, is a lesson plan that is very complete. It usually contains word for word what the instructor intends to say during the unit of instruction. This type of lesson plan is superior to the topic or sentence outline in that its detail ensures the coverage of all points in a consistent manner. Due to its completeness any research gathered by the instructor is preserved for future reference and can readily be used by replacement or substitute instructors.

On the minus side, the manuscript, or narrative, lesson plan is quite time consuming in the preparation process and requires a mastery of the language on the part of the instructor. Also, since this type of lesson plan contains the presentation practically verbatum, there is a tendency for the instructor to read from it, and it has a tendency to cause less preparation on the instructor's part before entering the classroom. Finally, because of its nature this type of lesson plan can discourage the students from taking meaningful classroom notes. As previously mentioned, many students have learned to organize classroom notes following an outline format and restructuring a narrative presentation to follow an outline format can be rather difficult unless the student is experienced in taking notes.

In selecting the lesson plan format to be followed there are several factors the instructor should consider. The first of these involves selecting a lesson plan format that will permit the attainment of the objectives stated for the unit of instruction. The lesson plan selected should also ensure the subject matter is presented in a logical learning sequence; that is, the material is presented in its proper sequence.

In addition to the above, the lesson plan should do several things for the instructor. It should provide a time line for the presentation so the instructor knows how much time of the total available he can expend on the various points within the presentation. The lesson plan should also indicate to the instructor the various teaching methods and procedures he plans to incorporate into the presentation. In conjunction with indicating the teaching methods or procedures the lesson plan should indicate the training aids that are to be used during the presentation and where they are to be used. Finally, the lesson plan should provide the instructor with a record from which examination questions can be drawn. In this regard, the instructor should teach from the lesson plan and not teach the anticipated examination questions.

In organizing the lesson plan there are several parts or elements to consider. The first of these is the title for the unit of instruction. While mentioning the title may seem simplistic there are several factors to consider when labeling a unit of instruction. The title should be a short heading that serves to indicate to the student what the unit of instruction will cover. It should be specific in nature and the use of ambiguous, unknown, misleading or controversial terms should be avoided in constructing the title.

The next part of the lesson plan, the statement of objectives, is one that requires the careful attention of the instructor. The statement of objectives essentially is a list setting forth, in specific terms, what is to be accomplished during the unit of instruction. These objectives should define the scope of the unit of instruction and be stated in terms of the exact knowledge, skills or attitudes which the instructor desires to impart to the students. The most common mistake made in conjunction with formulating these objectives is for. the instructor to state them in terms of his behavior rather than student behavior. If the objectives are to be meaningful to the student they must relate to his behavior, not the instructor's. By stating the objectives of the unit of instruction the instructor is telling the students what they can expect to learn as a result of the lesson.

Most of the lesson plans will contain information that is presented directly to the students, however, such is not the case with the next element, materials. The materials section of the lesson plan should be divided into two parts: training aids and references. The training aids portion is a listing of the various training aids to be used during the course of the presentation and can serve as a check-off list for the instructor as he prepares for the unit of instruction. In the references portion there should be a complete listing of the source materials used in developing the lesson plan. This list of references not only serves to authenticate the lesson plan but also allows the instructor to refresh his memory on the subject matter whenever necessary. Finally, both of these portions of the materials section can be extremely useful to the substitute instructor who is called upon on short notice to present the unit of instruction.

We have now reached that portion of the lesson plan that begins the actual presentation of the major portion of the unit of instruction, the introduction. The purposes of the introductory portion of the lesson plan are as follows:

1. To allow the instructor to identify himself and to state his particular qualifications for teaching the subject matter.
2. To point out the specific benefits the students can expect to

receive from the presentation, i.e. the statement of the objectives for the unit of instruction.

3. To establish a common ground between the instructor and the students.
4. To obtain and hold the attention of the class.
5. To relate this unit of instruction to the other units of instruction and to the entire course.
6. To establish within the students a receptive attitude toward the subject matter.
7. To lead into the development of the lesson itself.

Several techniques may be employed during the introductory portion of the lesson plan to satisfy the previously listed purposes. The first of these is called the attention step and serves exactly that purpose, to gain the attention of the class. The attention step could consist of a story or incident, an unexpected or surprising statement or the asking of a question that helps to relate the subject to be examined to the students' needs. For example: if the subject matter was traffic stops the presentation might begin with a newspaper account of how a police officer was assaulted on a *routine* traffic stop; if the subject was the police officer's use of a deadly force it might begin with the question, "Why should police officers be armed?"

Another technique that may be used during the introduction is the motivation step. This step should offer specific reasons for the student to be familiar with, to know, to understand, to apply or to be able to perform the material contained in the presentation. It is important that the reasons offered be of such a nature that they appeal to each student on a personal basis in relation to career advancement, financial gain or personal satisfaction.

The final step to be used during the introduction is the overview step. This step should clearly and concisely tell the students what is to be covered during the presentation. In addition, the overview step should relate past and future units of instruction to the one that is about to begin.

Once the introduction portion of the lesson plan has been completed the next element of the lesson plan, the development of the lesson, comes to the fore. The development of the lesson is the logical presentation of the subject matter to be examined during the unit of instruction. The term *logical* is extremely significant in this context in that the subject matter should be presented in its logical learning sequence. Some of the common methods used during the development of the lesson to present the material in a logical learning sequence are as follows:

1. From the past to the present or from the present to the past. For example: if the unit of instruction was concerned with the rights of those under arrest, the presentation might begin with a statement of those rights and develop into a discussion as to why court rulings have caused these rights to come into prominence. Conversely, the presentation might begin with the historical development of such rights and conclude with an explanation of the rights themselves.

2. From the simple to the complex. For example: if the unit of instruction was concerned with the officer-violator relationship, the presentation might begin with the typical contact resulting from a traffic stop and proceed to those situations where the officer is confronted with an abusive, argumentative or intoxicated violator.

3. From the known to the unknown. For example: if the unit of instruction was concerned with making speed estimates based upon skidmark evidence the presentation might begin with a review of skidmark evidence and proceed into an examination of the equations used to determine speed based upon skidmark evidence.

4. From the frequently used to the least frequently used. For example: if the unit of instruction was concerned with report writing the presentation might begin with an examination of the forms or reports within the organization that are frequently used, such as the uniform traffic ticket, and proceed into an examination of the less frequently used forms relating to traffic enforcement, such as the alcoholic influence report form.

In the process of developing the lesson the instructor should develop a series of major points and then, under each major point, develop a series of subordinate or supporting points. These subordinate or supporting points should relate to each other and lead to a complete understanding of the major point.

The last element in the lesson plan is the conclusion of the lesson. This element of the lesson plan contains three important segments that are frequently overlooked or de-emphasized even by the most experienced instructor. Usually a poor conclusion to the presentation results from the inappropriate usage of time on the part of the instructor. His poor use of available time results in his reaching the point in the presentation where the conclusion is appropriate and discovering no time remains.

The first element in the conclusion of the lesson is the summary. The summary should be used by the instructor to review or restate the major points that were presented during the lesson. In most presentations of longer than one hour it is likely the students will forget some of the major points explained during the initial phase of the presentation. This summary affords the student an opportunity to refresh in his mind these important points and also provides him with an opportunity to review his notes to ensure their completeness and accuracy. During this summary the instructor should be careful not to insert any new material that was not part of the just completed presentation. The insertion of new material into the summary leads to confusion in the students' minds and may well generate a discussion for which no time remains.

Along with a summary, the conclusion of the lesson should contain a remotivation step. Just as the introduction contains a motivation step to indicate to the students how they may personally benefit, the remotivation step exists to motivate the students into applying what they have learned during the presentation to their day-to-day job performance.

The final element in the conclusion of the lesson should be an appropriate closure. The closure consists of nothing more than thanking the students for their attention and involvement during the presentation. In addition, the closure might include an offer on the part of the instructor to provide assistance whenever needed.

Finally, in preparing a lesson plan you will find the preparation and resulting presentation much easier if you follow these guidelines:

1. Write out each of the major points you intend to cover during the presentation.
    a. Try to keep this number of major points at a minimum. One of the biggest mistakes an instructor can make is to attempt to present too much material in the time allotted.

b. Add supporting or subordinate material to each of the major points listed.

2. For each part of the presentation clearly indicate the method or technique of instruction you plan to use.

3. Make notations at the proper places in the lesson plan relating to illustrations, stories, experiences or statistical information that you plan to use during the the presentation.

4. At planned intervals in the lesson plan write out carefully worded questions designed to stimulate thinking and create discussion on the part of the students.

5. Indicate in the lesson plan the points when you plan to use audiovisual aids.

6. Establish and record a time schedule or time line for each element in the lesson plan and adhere to it as closely as possible.

7. Provide for a review or summary at the end of the presentation.

8. Prepare the testing device you will use to determine student achievement upon completion of the lesson.

In summary, the lesson plan is a guide to the instructor to be used during the presentation of a unit of instruction. It serves as the tool which enables the instructor to follow through with his carefully made plans to change the behavior of his students in accordance with his objectives for the unit of instruction.

Lesson plans are completed or prepared with several purposes in mind:

1. To ensure a wiser selection of material in keeping the instructor pointed toward the attainment of his objectives.

2. To provide the instructor with a logical and sequential presentation.

3. To provide for time control.

4. To indicate the methods and procedures to be used during the presentation.

5. To serve as a record for preparing examinations.

6. To give the instructor confidence during the presentation.

7. To refresh the memory of the instructor and to ensure important points are being covered.

A properly prepared lesson plan should contain the following elements:

1. Title.

2. Statement of objectives.

3. Materials.
4. Introduction.
    a. The attention step.
    b. The motivation step.
    c. The overview step.
5. Development of the lesson.
6. Conclusion of the lesson.
    a. Summary.
    b. The remotivation step.
    c. Closure.

# Chapter VIII

# EVALUATING TRAINING PROGRAMS

ONE of the most important responsibilities facing the training officer · is the evaluation of departmental training programs. Through this evaluation the training officer is able to identify the strengths and weaknesses of the training programs involving departmental personnel. It would be idealistic to assume each training program involving departmental personnel will fully satisfy the particular needs of the organization. Each training program, irrespective of how it is developed, who develops it or how it is presented, will have its deficiencies. These deficiencies may be the result of inadequate time, a lack of materials, a lack of funds, poor instruction or unrealistic goals or objectives for the course or individual units of instruction. In addition, each training program will also have its strengths which the training officer can take pride in and from which he may learn.

As previously mentioned, the goals or objectives set for the training program are one of the yardsticks whereby the effectiveness of the program may be measured; however, they do not constitute the only measuring device. Generally speaking, the goals or objectives of a training program will be expressed in rather general terms while the goals or objectives for the individual units of instruction will be framed in more specific terms. The evaluation of a training program in terms of its overall goals or objectives will probably result in the identification of some deficiencies; however, only the examination of the goals or objectives for the various units of instruction will result in identifying the specific nature of these deficiencies. For example: the goals or objectives of a training program in the field of firearms might be, "To acquaint the students with the proper range safety procedures and to develop in the students a proficiency with their personal sidearms as well as other special weapons."

This overall objective for the firearms training program is of a general nature in that it does not identify the proper range safety procedures, the precise degree of proficiency that is to be developed, what particular course or courses of fire are to be involved and what special weapons are to be used. These specific aspects of the training program will undoubtly be part and parcel of the overall training program, but they will be reflected in the goals or objectives for the individual units of instruction. If, during the evaluation process, it is determined that the graduates of the firearms training program are not displaying an adequate knowledge of range safety rules, one should then examine the goals or objectives for that particular unit of instruction. If these goals or objectives are properly stated, then perhaps the instructor and/or his method of instruction should be subjected to close scrutiny.

As a result of any training program, whether it be within or outside the organization, it is hoped the student will emerge with a new or refined set of skills and attitudes concerning the performance of his job. The manner in which he is able to apply these new or refined skills and/or attitudes then becomes the element that needs to be measured to determine the overall effectiveness of the training program. As a prerequisite to measuring these elements involved in job performance there should be developed job descriptions for each aspect of the job. A job description consists of a general listing of the performance requirements related to a particular task. Once a job description has been completed it will be necessary to complete a job analysis relating to the job. While the job description contains the performance requirements for a task, the job analysis contains a specific listing of the functions to be performed to complete the task in a satisfactory manner.

If, for example, the training had taken place in a particular area, such as accident investigation, then the job or task of accident investigation should be broken down into those tasks that comprise the accident investigation process such as:

1. Proceeding to the scene of the accident quickly and safely.
2. Parking properly at the scene of the accident.
3. Treating the injured and protecting their property.
4. Safeguarding the accident scene from further traffic accidents.

5. Determining if the accident is a hit and run case.
6. Locating and questioning the operators of the vehicles involved.
7. Locating and questioning any witnesses to the accident.
8. Noting all the physical evidence and conditions at the scene of the accident.
9. Taking photographs of the accident scene if necessary.
10. Inspecting and testing the vehicles involved in the accident for possible defects.
11. Determining the cause or causes of the accident.
12. Taking enforcement action against violations if warranted.
13. Clearing up the accident scene to prevent further accidents.
14. Following up on the nature and extent of personal injuries.
15. Writing the report containing the results of the investigation.

These then are the basic tasks the officer needs to perform in order to complete the investigation of the typical traffic accident. Each one of these tasks in turn also involves a related set of tasks. For example: the task of determining the cause or causes of the accident requires skills and knowledge relating to activities such as recognizing and measuring skidmarks, developing speed estimates based upon skidmark evidence, recognizing and evaluating the various types of vehicle damage, testing the vehicles involved for possible defects and evaluating their possible contribution to the collision and evaluating the effectiveness of traffic control devices, to mention a few. Prior to attempting any evaluation of a training program, one must be aware of the multitude of tasks that comprise a single element of any given job.

The measure of the effectiveness of training programs then is how well the student performs these tasks as compared to his performance prior to receiving the training? If he now performs all the tasks at a satisfactory level when he could not do so previously, then it can be stated the training program was successful and time well spent. In the event the officer's performance of some of the tasks is unsatisfactory after receiving the training, then this indicates the training program probably failed in that particular area. If so, then the training officer's job is to determine why the training program failed.

The process of evaluation is nothing more than determining at what level and in what areas you expect the student to be better able to perform than he could prior to having received the training. The more lengthy and general the nature of the training, the more difficult the evaluation process. The process of evaluating a training program for the recruit level officer will be much more difficult and time consuming than that of evaluating a specialized training program dealing with fingerprinting. This difficulty rests in the extensive and varied skills and knowledge required of the recruit level police officer.

Once the training officer has determined what is to be expected of the student in the way of performance as a result of the training program, he must select the processes and procedures to be used to measure the student's performance. One of these methods might cause the development of a form containing a breakdown of the tasks that comprise the elements of a job description. The immediate supervisor of the graduate is then requested to rate or evaluate the graduate officer's performance of the indicated tasks and to specifically note the nature of any deficiencies. Frequently mentioned deficiencies, involving most of the recipients of the training, relating to the same task would indicate a change in the training program would be in order since it appears all or most of the graduates are deficient in this area.

In the event these deficiencies occur infrequently and more or less at random and involve a minimal number of graduates, the indication is that the training program is basically sound. Deficiencies of this nature still indicate a need for additional training in the deficient areas. Training needs of this type could be met through coach-pupil or individual platoon or shift level training.

While the preparation of this list is the responsibility of the training officer, he should seek the advice and counsel of others within the organization when compiling the list. In particular, the advice of the first-line supervisor should be sought. Since the first-line supervisor deals on a day-to-day basis with the operational level employees' performance, he is in an ideal position to furnish information relating to the tasks involved in a particular job. In addition, other departmental personnel who become associated with or related to this job performance at a later date should be consulted as to what specific tasks comprise the job. This format should be followed by the training officer irrespective

of the element within the organization within which the evaluation is to take place.

When completing an evaluation of this type the supervisor
should base his comments on personal observations rather than
hunches or rumors he has heard concerning the officer to be
evaluated. In addition, the supervisor can and should solicit the
opinions of experienced, qualified officers who have had the
opportunity to observe the officer to be evaluated in the work
situation. These opinions should not be accepted as fact by the
supervisor but should serve to give direction to the nature and
scope of his personal observations. As previously mentioned,
problem areas or areas of deficiency should be mentioned in
specific terms rather than generalities.

For the sake of an example let us assume an officer has just
completed a basic or recruit level training program which included
a unit of instruction dealing with report writing. Let us further
assume his supervisor notes his reports generally contain all the
needed information, but they are sloppy in that they contain
numerous erasures, crossed out words and specific words are
constantly being misspelled. Noting deficiencies in this manner
will enable the officer to take the proper corrective action and
allows the training officer to determine exactly where his training
programs may need improvement. One of the prerequisites to
completing this evaluation is that the officer must be given
sufficient time to relate and apply what he has learned in the
classroom to his actual on-the-job experiences.

Another technique that may be used to evaluate the effectiveness of a training program is the questionnaire. Evaluation through
the use of this instrument requires very careful wording of the
questions so that the responses will be in specific terms rather than
generalities. Receiving a response stating a particular unit of
instruction, such as interviewing witnesses, was poorly presented
and little was to be learned indicates little to the training officer in
terms of what specifically is needed to remedy the situation.
Questionnaires of this type should be given to each graduate of the
training program after they have been removed from it long
enough to relate their on-the-job experiences to what they have
learned, or were expected to learn, as a result of the training

program. Unless the graduate has something to relate his or her training to, he cannot be expected to make valid judgements concerning its adequacy or inadequacy.

Finally, the questionnaire should not be used as the sole measure of the effectiveness of a training program. The questionnaire is too difficult to construct and the responses are usually too general in nature to be used as the only evaluation instrument. The questionnaire is most effective when used in conjunction with the supervisor's evaluation and the interview since both sides of the problem are available for examination.

The interview is the next type of device that may be used to evaluate training programs. The application of this instrument is accomplished by the training officer who interviews both the graduate of the training program and his immediate supervisor. The interview has one definite advantage over the other measuring instruments that have been mentioned. It allows the training officer, in the course of the interview, to press for and to receive specific information concerning the deficiencies and strengths within the training program. The major disadvantage to the interview as a measuring instrument is that it can be quite time-consuming. If time can be allotted for the interview procedure, then it will be time well spent.

Prior to the interview taking place the training officer should prepare a list of specific questions concerning the training received. For example: you would not want to ask the graduate officer what he thought of a particular unit of instruction, but instead ask him to explain, in detail, the procedures involved in the performance of a specific task that was included in the unit of instruction. As far as the officer's supervisor is concerned, he should be questioned as to how well the graduate officer performs these expected tasks. Once again, specific responses should be the order of the day.

As was the case in the previously mentioned evaluation techniques, it is advisable to allow some time to lapse between the termination of the training program and the interview situation. This will allow the supervisor time to observe and evaluate the officer on the job, and as previously mentioned, give the officer time to develop actual work experience to relate his training to.

All of these measuring instruments should be applied upon the termination of the training program. This does not mean the training program evaluation cannot take place during the program itself. Some of the deficiencies noted as a result of the application of either the supervisory evaluation, the questionnaire, or the interview can be traced directly to the instructor conducting the unit of instruction. It may well be that, as structured in terms of goals or objectives and time allotted, the training program is relatively free of defects. Irrespective of how well the training officer carries out his other duties and responsibilities, a poor or incompetent instructor can undermine an entire training program.

Instructor evaluation involves several steps, the first of which relates to the goals or objectives of the particular unit of instruction. Prior to actually preparing for the instruction the instructor and the training officer should meet and agree upon realistic goals or objectives for the unit of instruction within the time allotted. Once these goals or objectives have been agreed upon the instructor should prepare a lesson plan outlining how he is going to achieve these goals or objectives. This outline should then be reviewed by the training officer and the instructor to ensure its adequacy in terms of meeting the goals or objectives.

The next step is for the training officer to monitor, on an irregular basis, the class material as presented by the instructor to determine:

1. Does he follow his planned presentation as set forth in the teaching outline?
2. Is the instructor able to apply the various techniques of instruction in presenting the subject matter?
3. Is the instructor able to hold the attention of the class throughout the entire unit of instruction?
4. Does the instructor stimulate class discussion and participation?
5. Does the instructor use all the available resources, in terms of instructional aids, that are available and apply to his presentation?
6. How does the class react to the instructor's presentation in general?
7. Does the instructor structure his presentation to attain the prestated goals or objectives for the unit of instruction?

In other words, the training officer is in the classroom to determine how competent the instructor is and how well the class responds to his presentation. If it is later determined the training program was deficient in an area, and if the units of instruction have been minitored, the training officer can establish whether or not it was the fault of the instructor.

Another method that can be used to measure the class content and instructor ability is the class critique. Rather than having the critique completed by the class members upon completion of the training program. have them completed at the end of each block of instruction. In other words, a unit of instruction might involve ten hours relating to the rules of evidence by one particular instructor. Have the class critique the subject area and the instructor upon completion of the ten hours. The distinct advantage to completing the critiques at this time is that the impressions are still fresh in the minds of the students, and they are therefore less inclined to confuse instructors and subject material.

Only through evaluation can the training officer hope to refine and improve his training programs. If the training officer has designed a training program to meet a specific need, then the training program must be measured against that need. Training that does not meet the identified needs becomes training merely for the sake of training and serves to reduce the effectiveness of other departmental training efforts.

In summary, the evaluation of any training program must be in terms of the goals or objectives of that training program. In addition to using the overall course goals or objectives to evaluate the course, the goals or objectives of the individual units of instruction should be involved in the evaluation process. The evaluation process should not only be concerned with the content of the course itself, but also with those responsible for presenting the subject matter. Essentially there are three techniques the training officer may use during the evaluation process: the supervisory evaluation of the graduate officer, the questionnarie and the interview. Remember, in all instances the graduate officer must be given sufficient time to relate and apply what he has learned in the classroom to his on-the-job experiences.

# BIBLIOGRAPHY

Crockett, Thompson S.: Law Enforcement Education 1968. Washington D.C., International Association of Chiefs of Police, 1968.

Kassoff, Norman C., Nickerson, John M., and Pillsbury, Kenneth: The State of the art. The Police Chief, 35:75, 1968.

The President's Commission on Law Enforcement and Administration of Justice: Task Force Report: The Police. Washington D.C., U.S. Government Printing Office, 1967.

☆ ☆ ☆ ☆ ☆ ☆ ☆ ☆ ☆ ☆ ☆ ☆ ☆ ☆ ☆ ☆ ☆

# COACH-PUPIL TRAINING CHECKLIST

| Subject Area | Explained | Dates Demonstrated | Practiced |
|---|---|---|---|
| I. Personal items. | | | |
|   A. Police and public. | | | |
|     1. Do not congregate or loiter at crime scenes, coffee shops, stores, etc. | | | |
|     2. Contacts with women. | | | |
|     3. Driving habits. | | | |
|     4. Full uniform worn correctly. | | | |
|   B. Command presence and courtesy. | | | |
|   C. Use of precaution, prepared for anything. | | | |
|   D. Personal conduct. | | | |
|     1. Smoking in public. | | | |
|     2. Offensive mannerisms and gestures. | | | |
|     3. Voice and word usage | | | |
|   E. Nonacceptance of gratuities and rewards. | | | |
|   F. Rapport with fellow officers and supervisors. | | | |
| II. Preparation for patrol. | | | |
|   A. Personal appearance and hygiene. | | | |
|   B. Uniform and equipment check and maintenance. | | | |
|   C. Information necessary for patrol. | | | |
|   D. Roll call procedures. | | | |

| Subject Area | Explained | Dates Demonstrated | Practiced |
|---|---|---|---|

|  | | Dates | |
|---|---|---|---|
| *Subject Area* | *Explained* | *Demonstrated* | *Practiced* |

E. Patrol vehicle and equipment inspection.
F. Servicing the patrol vehicle.
III. Arrest procedures.
   A. When to effect an arrest (search and seizure).
   B. How to effect an arrest.
      1. Difference between a felony and a misdemeanor.
      2. The use of force.
      3. Using the nightstick and handcuffs.
      4. Using MACE.
      5. Using the service weapon.
      6. Legal and moral aspects of shooting.
   C. How to search a person (male or female) in the field and in the jail or lockup.
   D. Resisting arrest (elements required).
   E. Removing occupants from vehicles.
   F. Information gathered at the time of arrest.
   G. Transporting prisoners to the station.
      1. Using the patrol vehicle alone and with another officer.
      2. Extra precautions for certain types of prisoners.
   H. Do not recommend attorneys or bail bondsmen.
   I. Prisoners' property control procedure.
   J. Booking and searching procedures at the station

| Subject Area | Explained | Dates Demonstrated | Practiced |
|---|---|---|---|

K. Handling prisoners in the detention facility.
L. Proper clearances and release procedures.

IV. Use of the police radio.

  A. Use of the car radio. It is suggested that the coach do all the transmitting for the first few days until the pupil understands the proper use of the radio.

  B. Radio technique.

    1. Proper position to hold the microphone.

    2. Use a normal voice.

    3. When out of the car, place the microphone where it is readily available.

    4. Be aware of the status of other cars. If another officer has something important happening, do not use the radio except in emergencies.

    5. Keep the dispatcher informed of your status.

    6. Learn the radio code, phonetic alphabet and unit identification.

  C. Each pupil should be taken into the communications center for at least one eight hour period. The following should be noted:

    1. Show the pupil the multiple responsibilities of the communications personnel.

| Subject Area | Explained | Dates Demonstrated | Practiced |
|---|---|---|---|
|     a. Answering the telephone. | | | |
|     b. Police radio. | | | |
|     c. Agencies monitored. | | | |
|     d. Alarm console. | | | |
|   2. Explain the teletype machine and general procedures. | | | |
|   3. Explain the proper use of the following: | | | |
|     a. Suspended operator file. | | | |
|     b. Emergency business data file. | | | |
|     c. Warrant file. | | | |
|     d. Teletype file. | | | |
|     e. Stolen bicycle file. | | | |
|     f. Briefing board. | | | |
| V. General operating procedures. | | | |
|   A. Use of the officer's notebook. | | | |
|   B. Field interrogations. | | | |
|   C. Questioning witnesses. | | | |
|   D. Statement taking. | | | |
|   E. Obtaining descriptions of property. | | | |
|   F. Obtaining descriptions of persons. | | | |
|   G. Report writing. | | | |
|   H. Follow-up investigations. | | | |
|   I. Protecting a crime scene. | | | |
|   J. Evidence procedures. | | | |
|   K. Using first aid. | | | |
|   L. Obtaining ambulances, tow trucks, fire apparatus. | | | |
|   M. Taking a dying declaration. | | | |
|   N. Checking permits and licenses, buildings, liquor establishments, etc. | | | |

| Subject Area | Explained | Dates Demonstrated | Practiced |
|---|---|---|---|
| VI. Officer's responsibilities. | | | |
| A. Purposes of patrol and general responsibility. | | | |
| B. Responsibility for crime, traffic and vice conditions on the beat. | | | |
| C. Departmental policies and procedures effecting the officer. | | | |
| D. Types of police patrol. | | | |
| E. One man patrol operations. | | | |
| F. Patrol methods and techniques, all shifts. | | | |
| G. Knowledge of the beat; places, persons, vehicles, property, geography and situations. | | | |
| H. Observation and perception on patrol. | | | |
| I. Developing contacts. | | | |
| J. Handling of civil matters. | | | |
| K. Relations with the public; prejudices, attitudes, etc. | | | |
| L. Relations with your immediate supervisor. | | | |
| M. Relations with command personnel. | | | |
| N. Relations with investigative personnel. | | | |
| O. Relations with other governmental agencies. | | | |
| P. Conduct and behavior. | | | |
| Q. Requests for assistance. | | | |
| R. Duties in emergency situations. | | | |
| S. Knowledge of the year, makes and models of automobiles. | | | |
| VII. Driving techniques. | | | |
| A. Proper driving habits. | | | |
| 1. Public opinion regarding disobeying traffic laws. | | | |

| Subject Area | Explained | Dates Demonstrated | Practiced |
|---|---|---|---|
| 2. Defensive driving. | | | |
| 3. Driving in inclement weather. | | | |
| 4. Proper parking. | | | |
| 5. Signaling. | | | |
| B. Answering routine, nonemergency calls. | | | |
| C. Identification and apprehension of traffic violators. | | | |
|    1. Stopping violators so as not to obstruct other traffic. | | | |
|    2. Use of the red light, siren and spotlight. | | | |
|      a. Daylight. | | | |
|      b. Darkness. | | | |
|    3. Positioning the patrol car in relation to the violator. | | | |
|    4. Approaching the violator's car. | | | |
| D. Stopping stolen or wanted vehicles. | | | |
|    1. Obtain assistance and position them before making the stop. | | | |
|    2. Positioning the patrol car in relation to the suspect vehicle. | | | |
|    3. Approaching the suspect vehicle. | | | |
|    4. Removing the occupants from the suspect vehicle. | | | |
| E. Pursuit driving. | | | |
| F. Tailing suspects. | | | |
| G. Driving and parking in emergencies. | | | |
|    1. What constitutes an emergency. | | | |

| Subject Area | Explained | Dates Demonstrated | Practiced |
|---|---|---|---|
| 2. Using the red light and siren. | | | |
| 3. How to approach a burglary in progress call. | | | |
|   a. Proper procedures for a suspect at the scene or running away. | | | |
|   b. How to approach the assigned position. | | | |
|     (1) Need for lights out. | | | |
|     (2) Eliminate noise. | | | |
|     (3) Direct or indirect approach to scene. | | | |
| 4. How to respond to robbery in progress calls. | | | |
| 5. How to proceed when assigned to a fire. | | | |
| VIII. Patrol procedures. | | | |
| A. Inspectional procedures and techniques. | | | |
|   1. Commercial establishments. | | | |
|   2. Vacation house checks. | | | |
| B. Open windows and doors. | | | |
| C. Finding a burglary, search of the premises. | | | |
| D. Residential burglary in progress. | | | |
| E. Robbery in progress | | | |
| F. Bank alarm. | | | |
| G. Suspicious persons or prowler calls. | | | |
| H. Searching yards and alleys. | | | |
| I. Roadblocks and observation points. | | | |
| J. Searching quadrant. | | | |
| K. Man with a gun calls. | | | |
| L. Conducting a raid. | | | |

| Subject Area | Explained | Dates Demonstrated | Practiced |
|---|---|---|---|
| M. Crowds, mobs and riots. | | | |
| N. Demonstrations. | | | |
| O. Strike duty. | | | |
| P. Bomb threats. | | | |
| Q. Guarding prisoners. | | | |
| R. Transporting prisoners. | | | |
| IX. General investigations. | | | |
|   A. Patrol functions at felonies. | | | |
|   B. Preliminary investigation of a felony. | | | |
|   C. Modus operandi. | | | |
|   D. Investigation of murder, rape and assault. | | | |
|   E. Investigation of a robbery. | | | |
|   F. Investigation of burglaries. | | | |
|   G. Investigation of a safe burglary. | | | |
|   H. Investigation of a car theft. | | | |
|   I. Investigation of occupied suspicious vehicles. | | | |
|   J. Investigation of thefts. | | | |
|   K. Investigation of thefts from an auto. | | | |
|   L. Investigation of bad checks. | | | |
|   M. Investigation of frauds. | | | |
|   N. Investigation of embezzlements. | | | |
|   O. Investigation of extortion. | | | |
|   P. Investigation of suicides or unexplained deaths. | | | |
|   Q. False police reports. | | | |
|   R. Crime scene measurements and sketching. | | | |
|   S. Crime scene photography. | | | |
| X. Traffic procedures. | | | |
|   A. Police officers responsibility for traffic safety. | | | |
|   B. Pertinent traffic laws and ordinances. | | | |
|   C. Uniform traffic summons. | | | |

| Subject Area | Explained | Dates Demonstrated | Practiced |
|---|---|---|---|
| D. Selective enforcement. | | | |
| E. Recognizing traffic violations. | | | |
| 1. Evidence necessary for a conviction. | | | |
| 2. Moving violation. | | | |
| 3. Equipment violation. | | | |
| F. Approaching and handling the traffic violator. | | | |
| G. Enforcement techniques. | | | |
| 1. Use of the verbal warning. | | | |
| 2. Use of the summons. | | | |
| 3. DUIL arrests. | | | |
| 4. Use of the warrant. | | | |
| H. Parking violation enforcement. | | | |
| I. Traffic crash investigation. | | | |
| 1. Treating injuries. | | | |
| 2. Protecting the scene. | | | |
| 3. Locating drivers and witnesses. | | | |
| 4. Statements from drivers and witnesses. | | | |
| 5. Photographing, measuring and sketching the crash scene. | | | |
| 6. Determining the cause or causes of the crash. | | | |
| J. How to recognize and handle the drunk driver. | | | |
| 1. Observations. | | | |
| 2. Sobriety report. | | | |
| 3. Chemical testing. | | | |
| K. Hit and run traffic crash investigation. | | | |
| 1. Classification of the crash car vs. object. | | | |
| 2. Physical evidence left at the scene. | | | |

| Subject Area | Explained | Dates Demonstrated | Practiced |
|---|---|---|---|
| 3. Locating witnesses. | | | |
| 4. Notify other units of the suspect vehicle. | | | |
| 5. Contact garage owners and repair shops. | | | |
| L. Pedestrian violations. | | | |
| M. Use of radar. | | | |
| N. Use of VASCAR. | | | |
| O. Vehicle identification number, vehicle registration and license number. | | | |
| P. Driver identification, operators license. | | | |
| Q. Traffic direction and control. | | | |
| 1. General techniques of traffic control. | | | |
| 2. Standing where clearly visible. | | | |
| 3. Traffic control at a street with and without signals. | | | |
| 4. At an accident scene. | | | |
| 5. Proper use of flares, safety vest, flashlights and other reflectorized equipment. | | | |
| R. Police emergency escorts. | | | |
| XI. Vice control. | | | |
| A. Prostitution cases. | | | |
| B. Gambling cases. | | | |
| C. Liquor law violations. | | | |
| D. Narcotics violations. | | | |
| E. Contraband. | | | |
| XII. Juvenile procedures. | | | |
| A. Juvenile involvement in crime. | | | |
| B. Gaining the respect and cooperation of juveniles. | | | |
| 1. Juvenile competency must be evaluated. | | | |
| 2. Female juveniles should | | | |

| Subject Area | Explained | Dates Demonstrated | Practiced |
|---|---|---|---|
| be talked to with a matron present, or possibly in the presence of her mother. | | | |
| 3. Neighborhood juveniles as a source of information. | | | |
| C. Use of the juvenile department. | | | |
| D. Handling selected cases. | | | |
| 1. Malicious mischief and BB guns. | | | |
| 2. Runaways. | | | |
| 3. Juvenile liquor law violations. | | | |
| 4. Glue sniffing. | | | |
| 5. Truancy. | | | |
| 6. Curfew violations. | | | |
| 7. Child neglect and unfit home cases. | | | |
| 8. Battered and abused child cases. | | | |
| E. Juvenile gangs. | | | |
| F. Relationships with the agencies involved with juveniles; schools, welfare, recreation, detention, etc. | | | |
| G. Transporting juveniles to station or detention facilities. | | | |
| 1. When, where, what documents are needed. | | | |
| 2. Notification of parents. | | | |
| H. Disposition of juvenile cases. | | | |
| I. Juvenile traffic violations. | | | |
| J. Missing and found children. | | | |
| XIII. Handling people. | | | |
| A. Questioning suspects. | | | |
| B. Obtaining statements from suspects. | | | |

| Subject Area | Explained | Dates Demonstrated | Practiced |
|---|---|---|---|
| C. Wanted persons. | | | |
| D. Car prowlers. | | | |
| E. Beggars, vagrants. | | | |
| F. Questioning complainants. | | | |
| G. Obtaining statements from victims. | | | |
| H. Questioning witnesses. | | | |
| I. Obtaining statements from witnesses. | | | |
| XV. Legal processes. | | | |
| A. Obtaining complaints. | | | |
| B. Search warrants. | | | |
| C. Arrest warrants. | | | |
| D. Extradition procedures. | | | |
| E. Serving subpoenas. | | | |
| F. Chain of evidence. | | | |
| G. Rules of evidence. | | | |
| H. Case preparation for court. | | | |
| I. Courtroom testimony and demeanor. | | | |
| XVI. Hazards. | | | |
| A. Types of hazards, streets, buildings, etc. | | | |
| B. How to detect and report hazards. | | | |
| C. Fire hazards. | | | |
| D. Crime hazards. | | | |
| E. Insecure premises. | | | |
| F. Traffic hazards. | | | |
| G. Protective devices. | | | |
| H. Defective conditions in public property. | | | |
| I. Live wires | | | |
| XVII. Animal complaints. | | | |
| A. Found animals. | | | |
| B. Wounded or injured animals. | | | |
| C. Dead animals. | | | |
| D. Animal bite cases. | | | |

| Subject Area | Explained | Dates Demonstrated | Practiced |
|---|---|---|---|
| E.  Rabid animals. | | | |
| F.  Dog complaints. | | | |
| G.  Cruelty to animals. | | | |
| VIII.  Citizens complaints. | | | |
|   A.  Vacation checks. | | | |
|   B.  Medical aid assistance. | | | |
|   C.  Requests for assistance. | | | |
|   D.  Lock outs. | | | |
|   E.  Landlord-tenant disputes. | | | |
|   F.  Mechanic and baggage leins. | | | |
|   G.  Failure to pay cases. | | | |
|   H.  Citizens arrest cases. | | | |
|   I.  Information and directions to citizens. | | | |
| XIX.  Information. | | | |
|   A.  General information needed by the officer. | | | |
|   B.  Sources of information available at the station. | | | |
|   C.  Obtaining record, warrant and vehicle checks. | | | |
|   D.  Information and assistance available from other official agencies. | | | |
|     1.  Local agencies. | | | |
|     2.  County agencies. | | | |
|     3.  State agencies. | | | |
|     4.  Federal agencies. | | | |
|   E.  Sources of information on the beat. | | | |
|   F.  Press relations. | | | |
|   G.  Use of the departmental library. | | | |
| XX.  Organizational procedures. | | | |
|   A.  Checking on and off duty. | | | |
|   B.  Days off. | | | |
|   C.  Overtime. | | | |
|   D.  Leaves of absence, vacations, emergency leave, etc. | | | |

| Subject Area | Explained | Dates Demonstrated | Practiced |
|---|---|---|---|
| E. Sick and injured procedures; on and off duty. | | | |
| F. Checking out supplies and equipment. | | | |
| G. Equipment and uniform regulations. | | | |
| H. Care of police vehicles. | | | |
| I. Repair and maintenance of police vehicles. | | | |
| J. Discharge of firearms. | | | |
| K. Disciplinary procedures. | | | |
| L. Investigation of complaints against sworn personnel; procedures involved. | | | |
| M. Performance evaluation. | | | |
| N. Outside employment rules. | | | |
| O. Damage to departmental equipment. | | | |
| P. Change of address and telephone number. | | | |
| Q. Appearance in civil cases. | | | |
| R. Criminal court appearance. | | | |
| XXI. Explain the use and/or preparation of the following forms: | | | |
| A. Daily activity sheet. | | | |
| B. Various field offense reports. | | | |
| C. Vehicle accident report. | | | |
| D. Arrest report, prisoner's property report. | | | |
| E. Traffic summons. | | | |
| F. Daily bulletin. | | | |
| G. Sick and compensatory time requests. | | | |
| H. Equipment and uniform damage report. | | | |
| I. Field interrogation report. | | | |

| Subject Area | Explained | Dates Demonstrated | Practiced |
|---|---|---|---|
| XXII. Unlisted items (to be entered by the coach). | | | |
| A. | | | |
| B. | | | |
| C. | | | |
| D. | | | |
| E. | | | |
| F. | | | |
| G. | | | |

# EVALUATION QUESTIONNAIRE

*DIRECTIONS:* In order to evaluate the effectiveness of the recent training program you attended your cooperation is requested in completing this questionnaire. Your frank, honest answers are the key to the effectiveness of the evaluation. There is no need to identify yourself anywhere on this questionnaire. Thank you for your cooperation.

1. Which of the units of instruction have enabled you to perform your job better than you could prior to receiving the training?

_____

_____

_____

_____

_____

_____

_____

2. How did the material presented in the units of instruction listed in question # 1 assist you specifically in improving your performance? EXAMPLE: If you felt the unit of instruction dealing with traffic crash investigation was of assistance indicate how it was; e.g. you now realize the importance of skidmarks and their use in estimating vehicle speed and know how to utilize skidmark evidence properly.

_____

_____

_____

_____

_____

_____

_____

_____

_____

_____

_____

_____

3. Which units of instruction did not assist you in improving your on-the-job performance?

_____

_____

_____

_____

_____

_____

4. What were the specific defects in the units of instruction listed in question # 3? EXAMPLE: Some of the specific defects might be: the material presented does not apply to field situations (indicate the specific areas that do not apply), i.e. the booking procedure as taught differs from the actual procedure; the instructor did not cite enough examples; or he was too hasty in his presentation.

_____

_____

_____

_____

_____

_____

_____

_____

_____

_____

5. What other circumstances, if any, contributed to your learning less from the material presented than you hoped to? EXAMPLE: Frequent interruptions in the classroom by outside personnel. Tests prepared improperly. Instructors inadequately prepared.

_____

_____

_____

_____

_____

_____

6. Which of the units of instruction presented should be expanded to include additional information and specifically what information should be included?

_____

_____

_____

_____

_____

_____

7. Which of the units of instruction presented should be reduced to eliminate nonessential material and specifically what information should be removed?

_____

_____

_____

_____

_____

_____

_____

8. What additional units of instruction should be added to the course to improve its overall effectiveness?

_____

_____

_____

_____

_____

_____

_____

9. If you were responsible for the course of instruction you just completed, what would you do, in addition to what has already been listed, to improve the course?

_____

_____

_____

_____

_____

10. Use this space to make any additional comments you have concerning either this recently completed training course or the department's training efforts.

_____

_____

_____

_____

_____

_____

_____

_____

_____

_____

_____

_____

_____

_____

_____

_____

_____

_____

_____

_____

_____

_____

_____

# SUPERVISORY EVALUATION FORM

**POSITION: DISPATCHER**

| Task | Comments |
|---|---|
| I. Radio | |
|    A. Operation of the microphone. | |
|    B. Knowledge of the call sign. | |
|    C. Brief, precise transmissions. | |
|    D. Promptly acknowledges units. | |
|    E. Emergency broadcast procedures: | |
|       1. Net cleared? | |
|       2. Unit locations determined? | |
|       3. Primary and secondary assignments made? | |
|       4. Adequate coverage at the scene? | |
|       5. Closest units assigned? | |
|    F. Identity of departments monitored. | |
|    G. Location of monitors. | |
|    H. Log. | |
|       1. Location of blank forms. | |
|       2. F.C.C. requirements. | |
|       3. Entries: | |
|          a. Transmissions to units. | |
|          b. Transmissions from units. | |
|          c. Complaint assignments. | |
|          d. Shift assignments. | |
|          e. Relief assignments. | |
|          f. Information received. | |
|    I. Location of base station | |
|    J. Location of emergency base station. | |
|    K. Location of emergency or standby generator. | |

| *Task* | *Comments* |
|---|---|

    L. Procedures for starting emergency gener-
        ator.

    M. Telephone number of radio repair ser-
         vice.

II. Telephone.

    A. Promptly answered.

    B. Properly answered.

        1. Identification of the department.

        2. Identification of self.

    C. Courteous response to caller.

    D. Knowledge of other departmental num-
        bers.

        1. Chief of Police

        2. Detectives.

        3. Shift commander.

        4. Command officers.

    E. Knowledge of city office numbers.

        1. Mayor, City Manager.

        2. City council.

        3. City clerk.

        4. Department of public works.

        5. Dog warden.

    F. Knowledge of emergency numbers.

        1. Gas company.

        2. Electric company.

        3. Water company.

        4. Fire department.

        5. Specialized governmental units.

    G. Ability to transfer calls.

    H. Refers nonlaw enforcement calls to the
        appropriate agencies.

    I. Ability to handle several calls simultane-
        ously.

    J. Terminates call properly.

        1. Thanks the caller for calling.

        2. Assures the caller of action when
           appropriate.

III. Files.

    A. Location of:

| Task | Comments |
|---|---|

1. Warrant file.
2. Field interrogation card file.
3. Teletype messages.
4. Master name file.
5. Stolen vehicle file.
6. Radio log file.
7. Complaint file.
8. Vacation house check file.
9. On-call list.
10. Vehicle registration file.
IV. Tactical plans.
  A. Location of.
  B. When used.
  C. Specific plans:
    1. Bank alarms.
    2. ADT alarms.
    3. Felony in progress.
      a. Armed robbery.
      b. Burglary.
      c. Murder.
      d. Assaults.
      e. Kidnapping.
    4. Bomb threats.
    5. Fires.
    6. Airplane crash.
    7. Natural disasters.
    8. Riots or civil disorders.
    9. Civil defense alert.
  D. Notifications required (when appropriate).
    1. Chief of Police.
    2. Mayor.
    3. City council.
    4. City Manager.
    5. Command officers.
    6. Shift commanders.
    7. Detectives.
    8. On-call personnel.
    9. Off-duty personnel.

| Task | Comments |
|------|----------|
| 10. Specialized personnel.<br>11. Fire department.<br>V. Teletype.<br>   A. Location of.<br>   B. How used:<br>      1. Interstate.<br>      2. Intrastate.<br>      3. Interdepartmental.<br>      4. Information.<br>   C. Location of spare paper.<br>   D. Telephone number of repair service.<br>   E. Distribution of messages.<br>   F. Operation of the machine.<br>VI. Computor tie-in machines.<br>   A. Location of.<br>   B. Uses of:<br>      1. Wanted persons.<br>      2. Wanted vehicles.<br>      3. Stolen property.<br>      4. Drivers' records.<br>      5. Vehicle registration.<br>      6. Criminal records.<br>      7. N.C.I.C. interface.<br>   C. Message formats.<br>   D. Telephone number of repair service.<br>   E. Operation of the machine.<br>   F. Distribution of messages.<br>VII. Supplies.<br>   A. Location of:<br>      1. Radio log forms.<br>      2. Complaint log forms.<br>      3. Typewriter ribbons.<br>      4. Complaint forms.<br>      5. Blank typewriter paper.<br>      6. Lined paper.<br>      7. Pencils, pens, etc.<br>      8. Warrant file cards.<br>      9. Carbon paper.<br>     10. Supplemental report forms. | |

| Task | Comments |
|---|---|
| 11. Emergency notification forms. | |

VIII. Reports required of the dispatcher.
  A. Radio log.
  B. Complaint log.
  C. Teletype log.
  D. Computor tie-in log.
  E. Vacation house check cards.
  F. Stolen bicycle reports.
  G. Minor criminal complaints when no investigative leads exist.
  H. Emergency notification form.
  I. Defect forms relating to street lights, traffic control devices, roadways or security problems.
IX. Any performance areas not listed above.
  A.
  B.
  C.
  D.
  E.
  F.

☆ ☆ ☆ ☆ ☆ ☆ ☆ ☆ ☆ ☆ ☆ ☆ ☆ ☆ ☆ ☆

# INSTRUCTOR EVALUATION FORM

*INSTRUCTIONS:* Carefully evaluate the instructor in those areas as indicated. Indicate with a checkmark that descriptive phrase which best describes the instructor's level of achievement. Explanatory comments should be included whenever possible. Comments should be recorded whenever the instructor receives less than the highest rating.

| *Categories* | *Comments* |
|---|---|
| I. Introduction. | |
|     A. Unit objectives stated. | |
|     B. Attention getting step used. | |
|     C. Motivation step used. | |
| II. Knowledge of the subject. | |
|     A. Exceedingly well informed. | |
|     B. Adequately informed. | |
|     C. Not well informed. | |
|     D. Very poorly informed. | |
| III. Organization. | |
|     A. Extremely well organized. | |
|     B. Well organized. | |
|     C. Organization somewhat lacking. | |
|     D. Organization lacking. | |
| IV. Coverage of subject matter. | |
|     A. Excellent coverage. | |
|     B. Adequate coverage. | |
|     C. Poor coverage. | |
|     D. Coverage lacking. | |
| V. Ability to explain. | |
|     A. Explanations clear and to the point. | |
|     B. Explanations usually adequate. | |
|     C. Explanations often inadequate. | |

| *Categories* | *Comments* |
|---|---|

    D. Explanations totally inadequate.

VI. Attitude toward students.

    A. Sympathetic, helpful, concerned.

    B. Usually helpful and sympathetic.

    C. Avoids individual contact.

    D. Distant, cool, aloof.

VII. Attitude toward subject.

    A. Enthusiastic, enjoys subject.

    B. Rather interested.

    C. Only routine interest shown.

    D. Uninterested.

VIII. Training aids.

    A. Excellent usage.

    B. Adequate usage.

    C. Used, but ineffective.

    D. Not used.

IX. Use of lesson plan.

    A. As a guide.

    B. Follows objectives.

    C. Frequent reference to.

    D. Reads from lesson plan.

X. Questioning.

    A. Excellent use of oral questioning.

    B. Frequently questions class.

    C. Occasionally questions class

    D. Does not question class.

XI. Tolerance to disagreement.

    A. Encourages and values reasonable disagreement.

    B. Accepts disagreement fairly well.

    C. Discourages disagreement.

    D. Dogmatic, intolerant of disagreement.

XII. Summary.

    A. Effective coverage.

    B. No new material.

    C. Remotivation step used.

    D. No summary.

XIII. Instructor characteristics.

    A. Speaking ability.

| Categories | Comments |
|---|---|

      1. Voice and demeanor excellent.
      2. Adequate or average.
      3. Poor speaker—distracting.
      4. Poor speaker—a serious handicap.
B.  Class control.
      1. Maintains excellent class control.
      2. Adequate or average class control.
      3. Poor class control.
      4. Class control lacking.
C.  Rate of speech.
      1. Ideal for understanding.
      2. Adequate or average.
      3. Slightly too fast.
      4. Too fast for understanding.
D.  Eye contact.
      1. Excellent eye contact.
      2. Adequate eye contact.
      3. Limited eye contact.
      4. Eye contact lacking.
E.  Posture.
      1. Excellent posture.
      2. Average.
      3. Occasionally leans on objects.
      4. Constantly leans on objects.
F.  Use of gestures.
      1. Excellent usage.
      2. Frequently used.
      3. Occasionally used.
      4. Never used.
G.  Mannerisms.
      1. Has none that distract.
      2. Not too distracting.
      3. Hard to follow due to mannerisms.

| Dates Evaluated | Time Spent | Unit of Instruction |
|---|---|---|
|  |  |  |
|  |  |  |
|  |  |  |
|  |  |  |
|  |  |  |
|  |  |  |
|  |  |  |
|  |  |  |
|  |  |  |
|  |  |  |
|  |  |  |
|  |  |  |

Instructors name _____

# SAMPLE LESSON PLAN

Title: Preparation for instruction
Hours: One (1)
Method: Lecture, discussion
Materials: Chalk, chalkboard

I. Unit objective: Upon completion of this unit of instruction the student will be able to:
List the steps to be used in preparing for instruction.

|  | Time/Comments |
|---|---|
| II. Introduction<br>    A. The key to conducting a successful unit of instruction is preparation.<br>        1. The proper preparation enables you to realize the maximum learning efficiency in the time allotted.<br>        2. If you expect to be a successful instructor you cannot rely upon chance to accomplish this goal.<br>        3. If you fail in the instructional role you must accept the blame for this failure.<br>    B. As a general rule you should be prepared to present more material than the time allows.<br>        1. This rule applies particularly to initial presentations which are difficult to time properly.<br>        2. As experience in teaching a unit of instruction increases so should your ability to time the presentation. | 8 minutes |

| | *Time/Comments* |
|---|---|
| III. Planning the unit of instruction | 47 minutes |

III. Planning the unit of instruction

A. If a course objective has been established, determine how your unit of instruction fits into the overall objectives of the course.

B. Write or determine the objectives for your unit of instruction bearing in mind:
1. The course objective.
2. The time allotted in which to conduct the unit of instruction.
3. The composition of the class.
4. Physical facilities available.

C. If the objectives for your unit of instruction have already been established then structure your lesson plan to achieve these objectives.

D. Ensure that you have an adequate supply of the materials you intend to utilize during your presentation.
1. Audiovisual aids.
2. Handout materials.
3. Textbooks and other reference materials.

E. Study your material carefully.
1. Make certain that you have considered all aspects of the instructional process.
a. What method(s) of instruction do you plan to utilize during the course of the presentation?
b. How do you plan to integrate your training aids into the presentation?

F. Prepare a teaching content analysis.
1. A teaching content analysis is nothing more than a topical outline covering all the essential elements covered in the unit of instruction.
2. The teaching content analysis is a

| | Time/Comments |
|---|---|

guide to assist you in preparing your
lesson plan.
G. Prepare your lesson plan.
   1. Using your teaching content analysis
as a guide, detail the format you
intend to follow in conducting the
unit of instruction.
   2. Develop your lesson plan following a
logical learning sequence.
H. Rehearse your presentation.
   1. An absolute must if you are to
achieve the proper timing in your
presentation.
   2. Present your unit of instruction to a
live audience, such as your fellow
instructors or your family.
   3. Use a recording device to transcribe
your presentation and then listen to
the playback.
   4. Your rehearsal will probably reveal
the need to modify or change certain
aspects of the presentation. Make
certain these changes are made before
you present the material to the class.

IV. Summary                                5 minutes
A. Steps to be taken in preparing to conduct a
unit of instruction.
   1. Determine the course objectives.
   2. Determine or prepare the objectives
for your unit of instruction.
   3. Ensure that you have an adequate
supply of the materials you plan to
utilize in the course of your presentation.
   4. Study your material carefully.
   5. Prepare a teaching content analysis.
   6. Prepare a lesson plan.
   7. Rehearse your presentation.

|  | *Time/Comments* |
|---|---|

8. Modify your presentation as indicated by the rehearsal.
B. Remember, the objective of teaching is to achieve learning on the part of the students. Unless you properly prepare to assume the instructional role your classroom activities will result in failure.

# INDEX

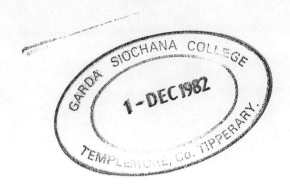